Half of What I Say Is Meaningless

The Will D. Campbell Award for Creative Nonfiction

The Will D. Campbell Award for Creative Nonfiction is given to the best manuscript that speaks to the human condition in a Southern context.

2010   Kathy Bradley, *Breathing and Walking Around*
(published 2012)

2011   No Award Given

2012   Joseph Bathanti, *Half of What I Say Is Meaningless*
(published 2014)

Half of What I Say Is Meaningless

Joseph Bathanti

MERCER UNIVERSITY PRESS
MACON, GEORGIA

MUP/ H880

Published by Mercer University Press, Macon, Georgia 31207
© 2014 by Mercer University Press
1400 Coleman Avenue
Macon, Georgia 31207

9 8 7 6 5 4 3 2 1

Books published by Mercer University Press are printed on acid-free paper that meets the requirements of the American National Standard for Information Sciences—Permanence of Paper for Printed Library Materials.

Library of Congress Cataloging-in-Publication Data

Bathanti, Joseph.
  Half of What I Say Is Meaningless / Joseph Bathanti. -- First Edition.
    pages cm
  ISBN 978-0-88146-473-3 (hardback : acid-free paper) -- ISBN 0-88146-473-2 (hardback : acid-free paper) -- ISBN 978-0-88146-490-0 (ebook) -- ISBN 0-88146-490-2 (ebook)
1. Bathanti, Joseph. 2. Authors--21st century--Biography. I. Title.
  PS3602.A89Z46 2014
  814'.6--dc23
  [B]
                                    2013045445

Contents

MERCER
UNIVERSITY PRESS

Endowed by
TOM WATSON BROWN
and
THE WATSON-BROWN FOUNDATION, INC.

For my dearest Marie – and in memory of our beloved parents,

Joe and Rose; and

in memory of my beloved mother-in-law, Rowena Carey Payne.

Acknowledgments

Many thanks to the following publications in which many of these essays originally appeared, occasionally in different versions:

"Maz's Homer" in *Aetholon: The Journal of Sport Literature*; "Thinking Big Budget: Twenty-Five Bucks and Two Cans of Bud" in *The Independent*; "Irony" in *Independence Boulevard*; "Irony" in *Kraut Kreek Revival*; "The Turf of Hankering" in *North Carolina Literary Review*; "Shuffletown" in *New Letters*; "Ghost, Come Back Again" in *Smoky Mountain Living*; "Blind Angels," "Ghostwriting," "Half of What I Say Is Meaningless," "Real Work," "This Bastard Day" and "Your Mum and Dad" in *The Sun*; "Ghost, Come Back Again" in *The Thomas Wolfe Review*; "Half of What I Say Is Meaningless" in *War, Literature and the Arts*.

Thanks also to the anthologies and their editors in which the following essays appeared:

"Half of What I Say Is Meaningless," in *Luck: A Collection of Facts, Fiction, Incantations and Verse*; "Your Mum and Dad" in *Picturing Texts*; "A Christmas Story" in *Tis the Season: The Gift of Holiday Memories*; "Ghost, Come Back Again" in *What Writers Do*.

"Ghost, Come Back Again" is the winner of The 2010 Donald Murray Prize, awarded annually by the National Council of Teachers of English.

What Really Happened:
Autobiography or Narcissism?

And so Narcissus, having come to a pool to quench his thirst, saw his reflection in its smooth surface, and fell in love with it. And since he could not obtain the object of his love, he died of sorrow by the same pool.

—Pausanius

Memory is the reservoir from which I write and I sit obsessively at the edge of that pool, like Narcissus, disturbing the waters again and again for the seductive flashes of the past that shape-shift and disappear each time I attempt to embrace them.

Writing and memory are grudge-holding Siamese twins not clearly on speaking terms. Yet, the writer, the autobiographical writer—and I find myself by default among his ranks—must reconcile himself to, and make peace with, his memory, if he is to write with any sustained vigor about his past. "Self-absorption," William Gass reminds us in the first sentence of his devilish diatribe, "The Art of Self: Autobiography in an Age of Narcissism," "is the principal preoccupation of our age."

Cautionary tales about memory and memoir are legend. There's no need to exhume James Frey or those wily memoirists who followed in his footsteps. We remain forever chastened. Nevertheless, at our fingertips exist hosts of comforting imprimaturs from many of our very best writers of contemporary creative nonfiction validating the genre's involuntary–and even wholly innocent—reflex to fabricate when memory falters. Patricia Hampl, for instance, in her extraordinary essay, "Memory and Imagination," says: "Invention is inevitable... each of us must have a created version of the past... We accept the humble position of writing a version rather than 'the whole truth.'" In commenting upon memoir, Joyce Carol Oates declares: "We are a species who clamors to be lied to."

Writers of creative nonfiction have a sacred office to tell the truth. Yet, while I remain troubled by our seeming inability to do so, I don't disagree with Hampl at all. At every turn, we are urged to strive for the "emotional truth." And what exactly is that? It's how you feel, isn't it? And doesn't it come down to *you, you, you*—"because," to quote Gass again, "we really believe in no other consciousness than our own." Narcissism, plain and simple—with the other foot mired in the sump of solipsism. Like Krapp, in Samuel Beckett's *Krapp's Last Tape,* we keep an obsessive eye on posterity. George Orwell famously shoots that elephant "solely to avoid looking like a fool."

I wish I could lay claim to a moral high ground, but I'm as guilty, more so, than most, of *invention.* I've always depended on falsehood. Paradoxically, when I first began writing in earnest, I was forced to abort every stab at fabrication, and acknowledge that I simply don't have the kinds of imaginations possessed by Don DeLillo, Margaret Atwood, Ray Bradbury, Tolkien or Ursula K. Le Guinn, of Edgar Allan Poe or even John Cheever. After countless false starts at imagining out of whole cloth brave new worlds, their citizens and accoutre-ments, I was forced to acknowledge that the only world, the only life, I could imagine (or *reimagine*)—that I had the range and trope to animate—was my own. Thus, as a way to get started, I turned my gaze inward, yet I found there no less bent toward exaggeration than had I been writing about lunar excavations.

Now, years and years beyond the actual (true) occasions that spawned the memoirs I choose to write, these written, often published, stories (because that's what they are—stories) have deposed memory, transposing themselves over what might have really happened. In fact, they have indeed become my memory. Mary Clearman Blew, in "The Art of Memoir," testifies: "...like the old Sunday storytellers who told and retold their stories until what they remembered was the tale itself, what I remember is what I have written."

In poems and fiction and plays, it doesn't matter if something actually occurred. The psychic and spiritual truth embodied in Shakespeare's *Hamlet* is not rendered moot should we discover that there really wasn't a Danish price named Hamlet. That revelation would not damage Shakespeare's credibility a whit nor the ineffable genius of his play. But should we discover that a war in *real life* (which in genre terms is the equivalent of creative nonfiction) has been predicated upon a fiction—the fiction, say, that a country is hoarding weapons of mass destruction and that invasion of that country and certain bloodshed is not only unavoidable, but honor-able—then we feel duped, outraged, betrayed. Sometimes it's okay to lie, and sometimes it isn't. What's more, depending on what genre the writer is engaged in, as well as his integrity as a writer and human being, he always knows the difference.

It's no secret that writing requires an abundant store of "self-absorption." But "self-absorption" has never been a burden for writers. To successfully explore an occasion in writing depends dramatically on the range of linguistic, narrative, and imaginative strategies congenial (and often harrowing) to writing about that occasion as it shape-shifts from genre to genre to genre. The beauty of poetry and fiction is that false-hood is tolerated; but, strange as it is, do not for a moment believe that your readers will not be aghast if they discover your fictions to be false. Poetry requires an elegant ear, the precision of a surgeon, and compressed, musical language. It's a "small" genre that can transform a near invisible speck into the entire illuminated universe, and has the wallop and collateral range of a hand grenade.

Fiction maintains a looser gait, yet a panoramic canvas. You can get away with more. The readership for fiction, as opposed to poetry, is exponentially wider, but in the ranks of that readership are hordes of amateurs with pronounced bad taste. There are very few amateur poetry readers, just as there are few amateur pole-vaulters. Thus a bad poem will instantly out itself to the habitual reader of poetry, whereas bad fiction is often permitted among its more pluralistic readership to masquerade as worthy indefinitely. Really fine fiction—and we all have our short lists—is really fine, and lasting, because its language is memorable and breathtaking. The best fiction is best because it aspires to the lyric integrity of poetry.

Creative Nonfiction—memoir specifically—remains the nitroglycerine of the three genres: rocking precariously in a rickety wagon driven by drunken mule skinners, pulled by drunken mules, along a mud-scarred, rocky, potholed road. Not only does creative nonfiction have to showcase the exquisite language of poetry, but it must also entertain in the vein of winning literary fiction and adhere to all of its conventions— plot, narrative, point of view, dialogue, characterization, dialogue, conflict, crisis, resolution. And its practitioners are not allowed to lie (willingly)—the ace in the hole of poets and fiction writers—for if they do they'll have the FBI and the CIA, and battalions of self-appointed fact checkers aiming to disgrace them. One false move, a sneeze, a fidget or flinch and they'll be blown to kingdom come. The only sleight of hand the writer of creative nonfiction is permitted is a great story and dazzling writing.

On the other hand, creative nonfiction is permitted the kind of digression I have indulged in throughout this piece—similar to Patricia Hampl's jarring time-out a third of the way into "Memory and Imagination" when she confesses that "the truth is, [she doesn't] remember" Sister Olive Marie, her piano teacher and a key character in her essay, "at all." Hampl then goes on to recant a number of other recollections that up until that moment in the essay, we, the audience, had taken for gospel. It is at that point that the fascinating memoir we thought we were reading metamorphoses into a fascinating epistle on craft. Such razzle-dazzle is prohibited in poetry and fiction. The playwright may not traipse out of the wings and rewrite the dialogue in mid-scene. This relatively recent phenomenon—memoirists conflating, within the same text borders, the memoir itself as well as companion craft commentary—is another hallmark of creative nonfiction's hybrid pedigree.

All anyone is trying to do is figure out what happened. Poignant stories begin with breathtaking ignorance—and most often, for me, in the catacombs of memory. It is a common hazard to idealize these burnished moments of the past—to even, God forbid, sentimentalize them. John Irving advises: "Please remember that all memoir is fiction." You don't even know if what I've told you is true. I suppose I don't either. I always thought Narcissus drowned, but he simply pined away.

The Turf of Hankering

On August 14, 1976, I drove for the last time as a Pittsburgh citizen over The Fort Pitt Bridge, ogling wistfully The Point—the nexus at which the Allegheny and Monongahela rivers form the Ohio, then push west into the vast imagination of America.

On the other side of the Fort Pitt Tunnels lay my destiny, another imaginary plain: the American South. I was 23, headed for Atlanta, Georgia and training as a brand new VISTA Volunteer, then off to North Carolina where I would work—doing what I had no idea—in the state's prison system despite knowing patently zero about prisons or jails, period, other than Humphrey Bogart, James Cagney and Edward G. Robinson movies. When I was a boy, and we chanced to drive by the gothic ornate city jail on Fifth Avenue in downtown Pittsburgh, or The Blockhouse, in Blawnox, armed guards pacing watchtower gantries, my father would simply gesture symbolically toward them.

Pittsburgh, my beloved home town, a place I had unconsciously invested with my own private mythos, was just punching out for the day, skyscraper windows golden from the sun reflected off the rivers, tugs and coal barges footling under massive bridges, the Gateway Clipper zipping its partygoers over the blinding green water. It never occurred to me that I might be leaving behind my identity. That I had already had a rich life seemed impossible.

I had gotten a late start, and my mother and father had urged me to postpone my departure until the following morning. But I had gassed up my wondrous first car, a 1969 Volkswagen Beetle, and made my goodbyes. I was burning to leave. My pockets were filled with friends' money I had won the previous night at a going-away poker game: a couple hundred bucks, what was left after I treated everyone at Ritter's, an all-night joint, after snagging the last pot. In the glove compartment was my Triple A trip-tick, courtesy of my dad, my route a jagged parabola from Pittsburgh to Atlanta highlighted in pastel blue.

My parents thought I was nuts for joining VISTA. My mother had been crying, off and on, for days. The only way to stop it was to beat it out of town. Through the rearview mirror, I studied them, waving from the porch of my boyhood home on 1410 Mellon Street, until they got smaller and smaller, and disappeared. Then I floored it.

As I drove over that bridge, and into the mouth of the south-bound tunnel, my former fellow construction laborers were sprucing up the site I'd toiled at all summer, racking my old hod into its stand, hosing down the mixers. I imagined my name stripped from the student mailboxes in the University of Pittsburgh's Cathedral of Learning, where I had just completed graduate school in English Literature. The Steelers were but a few weeks from launching their next Super Bowl campaign. *Goodbye, comrades,* I mused. *I'm headed South.*

The next day, August 15, The Feast of the Assumption—commemorating the taking up of Jesus's mother, the Blessed Virgin Mary, the Mother of God, body and soul, into heaven where she resides, world without end, its queen—I woke up in a Columbus, Ohio hotel, had breakfast, then got behind the wheel, the VW's $19.95 Earl Scheib paint job chipping in the ferocious onslaught of suicidal insects, more pronounced the further south I drove, the sleek black I had had it painted giving way to its original baby blue. Its sun roof was open. Despite the fact that the car lacked reverse gear—something that rendered it, and me, terrifically suspect in my already worried parents' eyes—it had been a constant, sturdy friend. We were rarely apart, and had travelled together as far as Miami, Bangor and all points between. There would be no turning back.

Sprawled heavily in the backseat, like a hung-over friend, was the footlocker my father and I had bought downtown two days before at the Army-Navy Store, sandwiched on Liberty Avenue by strip clubs, porno dives, and adult bookstores. Inside it were my effects, what would sustain me over the next weeks as I hatched out my new life: books and underwear, socks, flannel shirts, jeans, work boots, my baseball glove, and a new snap-button denim shirt my dad had inexplicably purchased for me. Dwarfed sheepishly next to the footlocker was an old Underwood typewriter in its cardboard carrying case.

Later that morning, I passed through Cincinnati, then crossed the prodigious Ohio River into Covington, Kentucky, and the invisible mythic Mason-Dixon Line. The Assumption is a Holy Day of Obligation, not only in Catholic Doctrine, but also in my own personal liturgical calendar—apropos of the stunning manner in which I *disappeared*, assumed by the Southland.

On I-75, outside Lexington, with its roiling long blue grass and black barns, a gleaming chrome Airstream, despite my flailing horn and my screaming through the open window, sidled determinedly into my lane and drove me off the road at 80 miles per hour. Our Lady was watching over me as she always has. There was no guard rail, or I would have been squashed, but a wide blue grassy median I careened through for half a mile before regaining control of the car. I sat there a moment, contemplating what a close call I had had. On either side of me, zooming juggernauts of steel and petroleum, rubber and smoke, combusted north and south. I was all alone, hundreds of miles from home, and feeling pretty good about it.

I listened to *Bookends* and *Abbey Road*, *Tea for the Tillerman*, over and over, on my prehistoric 8-track player bracketed under the dash. Through the Daniel Boone National Forest, over Cumberland Mountain and into the vast emerald Appalachians. Driving, singing, the wind throttling me through the opened windows, and peeled-back sun roof, there dawned a stunning realization: surrounded by the dizzying thrall of endless elevation, I was, in essence, nowhere. A fugi-tive. Between lives, coursing the ether. My past in Pittsburgh had been tied off like an umbilicus. How miraculous. I had been assumed.

At every milepost, it seemed, loomed signs for *Pedro's South of the Border*—a loony Mexican in giant sombrero and mustachioed beckoning leer—in Dillon, South Carolina. Stuckey's: where you could get boiled peanuts and pecan logs. The legends *Jesus Saves* and *John 3:16* hoisted on crude crosses towered out of the cropland, tattooed on fence posts and rail-heads. Jeremiads and spooky scripture chalked onto gray weathered barn-sides in a shadowy prehensile alphabet.

I longed to keep driving, but elected instead to bed down come nightfall on the shelf of the deep south, which Georgia signaled for me—perhaps to quell, for just eight hours more, my looming destiny. I checked into a motel in Cleveland, Tennessee, maybe forty miles northeast of Chattanooga, not far at all from the Chickamauga Battle field. Night had coated the steamy little town. Outside my curtained window I heard cicadas; crickets; traffic pummeling the interstate; moths flapping against the breezeway lights; the various settlings of lodgers and, above all, their polyphonous voices, independent of one another, yet each a stitch in an inscrutable story's weave.

I purchased the local newspaper, the *Cleveland Daily Banner*, alarming in its piety and repeated allusions to the Deity. I stared with some trepidation at the Gideon Bible on the nightstand. By the time I had finished watching on the black-and-white motel TV *The Four Horsemen of the Apocalypse*, I felt near evangelized. A young man's identity, on such a night, can slip away. I copped a gander at my Mediterranean mug in the fluorescent-lit mirror. My first beard sprouted in patches. *Man*, I thought, crawled into my sterile bed, and turned to page one of *Wuthering Heights*, *I really have come South*.

Any doubts about where I had landed were squelched irrevocably the next morning when I careened into Atlanta: the signature city of the new South, where it was all happening. *Atlanta* was on the lips of every hep cat I had run into back in Pittsburgh. The town in which Babe Ruth's canonical home run record was shattered by a black man, number 44, the magnificent Henry Aaron. Where Martin Luther King, Jr. laid down from the pulpit, and on the street, those Molotov Cocktail homilies that blew the dome right off the segregated world. I congratulated myself that I sat, amidst thrumming queues of automobiles fanned in every direction, in Atlanta's glittering molten heart. Vectors of heat ascended from the sidewalks, corrugating the troposphere out of which rocketed pods of opaline space age skyscrapers—mirrors and glass and chrome, the blinding light of the future. Nothing like *Gone with the Wind*.

I shielded my eyes and inched toward my destination: the Georgian Terrace Hotel on Ponce de Leon Street. I had directions, but quickly found myself confounded again and again in a tangle of Peachtree Streets. I parked my car and singled out an extremely old, cherubic-looking white-haired woman, hunched with age, strolling the burning sidewalk. Dressed head to toe in black, including a long-sleeved black cardigan, she nevertheless emanated a cool self-possession and whimsical smile.

What I knew about Ponce de Leon, himself, was that he had set out in search of the Fountain of Youth, which had perhaps taken him through what was now Georgia, and ended up discovering Florida. In asking the woman as to the hotel's whereabouts, I mentioned with great reverence and Frenchification—even though Ponce was a Spaniard—that its address was Ponce de Leon. The first thing she did was correct my pronunciation. Locals opt for a phonetic approach: *Ponsdaline*, to rhyme with and sonically mimic Valvoline, but with the least bit of a roll at the end, fusing those last two syllables, in what struck my ear as characteristically British—though the pitch and timbre of her voice were clearly a hybrid all its own: a decidedly authentic deep Southern drawl. She confided that she was out for a walk because she had been *hankering* for a bit of fresh air.

All I knew at the time about Southerners was what I had learned from television: *The Andy Griffith Show, Gomer Pyle, U.S.M.C., The Beverly Hillbillies.* Funny, occasionally charming, but with little ethnographic integrity. For native Southerners, those programs equaled what *The Jeffersons* represented for African Americans, what Jose Jimenez was for Latinos, what Ed Sullivan's little rodent buddy, Topo Gigio, was for Italian

Americans (though at the time, thank God, we called ourselves Italians). To put a charitable spin on things: perhaps those cartoons were that era's pathetic stab at multiculturalism, inclusivity.

I had, of course, seen *Gone with the Wind*. A nun had taught me *Dixie* in first grade music class. I knew by heart the theme song to *The Rebel*, a TV show starring Nick Adams as Johnny Yuma. I had heard legendary college football coaches Bear Bryant of Alabama, Frank Broyles of Arkansas, and Darryl Royal of Texas interviewed by sportscasters after bowl games—and I occasionally imitated, respectfully, I like to think, the Bear's accent. I had read Faulkner, Welty, McCullers, and O'Connor.

I grew up in a neighborhood where everyone was Italian, Catholic, first generation or newly arrived from the old country, and working class. Grandparents exclusively spoke Italian. Your dad was a brick layer, a cement finisher, or steel worker. There were a few chefs, a few tailors. Sunday dinner was sacramental: pasta. Growing up, I only knew people like me. It would not have occurred to me to think of myself as possessing a regional identity, and there was no evidence that the people I had grown up around thought any differently than I. We seldom, if ever, thought about Southerners, much like we didn't New Englanders, Midwesterners, or Westerners. I didn't even think of myself as a Pennsylvanian. I was from Pittsburgh—period (actually from East Liberty, my neighbor-hood, to put a finer point on it)—and the murky precincts of the rest my native state were irrelevant.

In fact, I never thought of myself as a Northerner until I moved to the South. By the time I made that move thirty-seven years ago, I had begun to think of myself as a writer, although it was more the *idea* of being a writer that I cherished, rather than the actual practice of writing. While my obsessive dream was to write, I had never truly engaged in the blue-collar enterprise of taking up my pen and making words on paper. Yes, I had frequently mistaken the muse for those delusionary transports wherein one scribbles wildly, certain, even smug, that the doggerel swill you're channeling is the real thing. But even these episodes were short-lived and months apart. I chose to emulate Sartre, figuring that by pretending to be a writer, I'd rather alchemically end up one. I also reasoned that a trek from home, which I had read had been essential for so many famous writers, would miraculously jar me into the consciousness necessary to what Flannery O'Connor called "the habit of being."

The day in 1976 I stood with that woman—who had begun to look so much like Eudora Welty—on one of Atlanta's Peachtree streets, I knew patently nothing about the South and its people. However, I was really quite innocent of thinking ill of them. Nevertheless, I would soon discover that Southerners, at least the 1976 vintage, held Northerners—Yankees to be precise—if not in contempt, then unvarnished suspicion.

When I arrived South, the Civil War still had a palpable valence—like an unburied body, its spirit not yet commended to sanctified ground: Polynices decomposing at the gates of Thebes. In Atlanta, if you squinted, you could make out—through that neo-Southern facade of glass, I-beams, neon, teeming commerce and traffic—the shades of slaughter crimped in the streets among flaming carnage. Folks seemed still seemed pretty pissed at Sherman. I had little context for this. For my people, there was another war, World War II—the one my father and uncles had all rushed off to—which, along with The Depression, I felt like I had vicariously lived through because it was incessantly talked about. But the Civil War? It was 1907 before my family reached the shores of America from Foggia. We had no dog in that fight—to invoke a Southern axiom.

It is perhaps interesting to point out, however, that as a child I received one Christmas a Civil War set: plastic armies of Union and Confederate soldiers, replete with canonry that really fired, and authentic exploding bunkers. Having for the first time arrayed the blue and gray troops in clear opposition, it dawned on me that I didn't know which side I was on. In other words: *Who should win?* I knew my cowboys were to annihilate the Indians, my Marines wipe out the Japanese. But this was different. Unable to make any clear ideological or ethnic distinctions between the two armies, I didn't know how to go about the killing. I liked the color blue better than grey, but this was not enough. I consulted my older sister, Marie. She informed me who *we* were. Thenceforth I saw to it, in varying degrees, that the North always triumphed.

But, actually, as I got older, I for some reason began to find the South rather exotic; and I once engaged one of my uncle's next-door neighbors—a woman recently relocated coincidentally from Georgia—in an inane conversation about croquet, about which I knew absolutely nothing, merely so I could listen to her talk.

That little old Eudora Welty lady: she couldn't quite direct me to the Georgian Terrace. "Bless your heart," she said more than once, a phrase I had never heard before, but would come to know well. She had also made repeated allusion to a personage I was soon to learn Southerners—waiters, bus drivers, cabbies, cops, lawyers, physicians, ditch diggers, and prison inmates (especially prison inmates)—talked about like the guy next door: our Lord and Savior, *Jesus*.

Suddenly I noticed the backdrop for our conversation: a skirmish of huge glass storefronts housing what, at first glance, I took to be nude and scantily attired mannequins. Then the mannequins inexplicably quickened and I realized they were not mannequins at all, but flesh and blood women—*naked* women, no less—on display, soliciting their wares, up and down a not-too-shabby city block of one of the Peachtree streets, Atlanta, Georgia. It was a, by God, storefront whore boutique. *Wow*, I thought, *this Bible Belt's something*.

And I was embarrassed. I wanted to throw my hands over the eyes of that dear Saint Eudora and spirit her away from such perfidy. But, of course, she knew what shimmied in those windows, and so did other passersby. That they were more practiced and pathological in their repression of it is key here. The whores, like Christmas trees, were beckoning to Johns from windows on Main Street, but if one ignored them, refused to acknowledge them, then of course they weren't there and could do no harm. This anecdote provides no useful scholarship on regional distinctions—or morality for that matter. My interest in it is merely as tableau—an unforgettable image. Counterpoint provides the writer with the best occasion for his craft.

I finally tracked down the Georgian Terrace Hotel, and pulled into its parking lot next to a car with a Pennsylvania license plate. A man and woman, my age, were just emerging from it. Turned out they were also VISTA recruits—from Pittsburgh, no less. Dave, an Italian, slight, with a skimpy black mustache, was actually from Greenburg, a small town maybe thirty miles east of Pittsburgh. In another epic coincidence, he ended up my VISTA roommate at the hotel. Patricia Bradshaw—pretty, blonde, tough, about six inches taller than Dave—had grown up in Penn Hills, a suburb, not three miles up the Allegheny from East Liberty, and had attended Penn Hills High School. She would have been in the stands when, as a senior football player for Pittsburgh Central Catholic, I had lost a heartbreaker on her home field. Her ancestry was Slovak; she had steelworker roots in Braddock where my dad was a millwright at The Edgar Thomson Works, Andrew Carnegie's inaugural American mill. Dave and Patricia, though not romantically connected, had also attended Indiana State College, a little state school north of Pittsburgh. I had a pair of Indiana State gym trunks in my footlocker.

The three of us, because of the Pittsburgh kinship, spent the evening together. We walked through the heart of the sweating space-age city to its famous Underground Atlanta, a far-out subterranean labyrinth of full-bore groove: clubs, bars, restaurants, honky-tonks with a decadent Dixie flair. In the 1920s, the city constructed concrete viaducts which raised its network of streets one storey to allow traffic to flow more efficiently. Merchants abandoned their suddenly underground storefronts, and relocated to the new upper level. Those original catacombs remained, unbeknownst, I presume, to the citizens of Atlanta, and in 1969 Underground Atlanta was unveiled.

We descended into the blinding vaults. I was bedazzled by its futuristic élan: tunnels of passing people, one cool joint after another, though the architecture of many of original storefronts remained. Carved granite, marble facing, cast iron and scrollwork, pilasters, archways. It had a Bourbon Street taboo about it: *noblesse oblige* and sin, hardly distinguishable, in the same

17

jigger. Everything about Pittsburgh seemed suddenly dismal and entrenched.

In the front window, literally, of Muhlenbrink's Saloon sat an old black albino guy, Piano Red, a local legend, at an upright banging out Blues and Ragtime. He wore a straw fedora. His skin was pink, his hair white. He closed his eyes as he sang, as if about to nod off. He gave the impression of being blind. We went in for beer and steak sandwiches. I was gratified that Dave and Patricia knew as little about what they'd signed onto in joining VISTA as I. I called my parents collect from a phone booth outside a fondue joint called Dante's Down-the-Hatch. I told them I was safe, having a good time and had already made two friends—from Pittsburgh, which I knew they'd find soothing.

On the way back to the hotel, we bought ice cream from a street vendor. In the still-stifling temperature, it dripped down the cones and into our hands. We passed the display harlots, sweating, pressing their breasts against the plate glass windows. What with the whores, the Southern heat, the fact that in a mere 24 hours I had travelled 700-some miles from home, I was a mite unraveled from the metamorphosis I was under-going, and took comfort in the presence of my Steeltown brother and sister.

Later that night, in the first hours of the morning, lying in the un-air-conditioned swelter of my hotel room, wearing only a pair of underpants, the last my mom had laundered for me, I was asked point-blank by my Pittsburgh roomie, Dave, if he could get in bed with me. I considered a number of responses and opted for a simple *No*. I was outraged, freaked. I was ready, if necessary, to start slugging; but I was also pleased. A story was writing itself.

The Georgian Terrace, at Peachtree and Ponce de Leon, struck me as a rococo hideout for pimps, prostitutes, junkies, outlaws, and brigands of all stripe—the kind of place my mother warned me to steer clear of. Derelicts lounged on the hotel's wide and deep front portico, a two story bank of windows behind them, smoking cigarettes like mad and swigging from bottles sheathed in brown pint paper bags (which I'd find out Southerners often called *sacks*), haranguing one another in Spanish as well as English as if warming up for a sizable brawl. In the sultry air hung the unmistakable scent of marijuana.

The place held for me an exotic, even charming, third-world seediness that I associated with the danger and romance of Bogart films set in Morocco. An interesting aside is that, in 1926, Bert Donaldson, the state of Georgia's chief investigator for the Solicitor General, was assassinated gangland style—both barrels of a shotgun—at The Georgian Terrace. His murder was attributed to a purported mob influence in Atlanta. The hotel, constructed of brick, marble and limestone, at a cost of a half-million dollars, opened for business on October 2, 1911 and would come to be known as the *Grand Old Lady of Peachtree*. By the time I ran into the Grand Old Lady in 1976, she had degenerated into a bit of a madame, but she still had the original coquettishness of her seductive beaux-Arts style. I liked her at once.

Directly across the street from her was The Fox Theatre, a lavishly ornate hall, originally the Yaarab Temple Shrine Mosque, that opened Christmas Day in 1929, less than two months before the Wall Street Crash. Often celebrities in town to perform at the Fox had stayed at the Georgian Terrace. When they departed the hotel, to walk across Peachtree to The

Fox, Atlanta police halted traffic and a long red carpet was literally spun from the hotel to The Fox to afford them a regal entrance into the theater. Mere weeks before I arrived in Atlanta, Lynyrd Skynard had played The Fox, and recorded live during its three-night-standing-room-only-run *One More From the Road*, leaving the stage on the third night after a standing ovation that followed their closer, "Free Bird"—but a year before the plane crash.

The public life, the phenomenon, of *Gone with the Wind* began at The Georgian Terrace. MacMillan editor, Harold Latham, who ended up looking rather clairvoyant when the novel won the Pulitzer in 1937, not to mention the unfathomable uproar of the film in 1939, and its subsequent canonization as the greatest film of all time—a perch it could be argued it still occupies—secured the unfinished manuscript from Margaret Mitchell, then Peggy Marsh, in the lobby of the Georgian Terrace in 1935. What's more, many of *Gone with the Wind's* luminaries quartered at the Georgian Terrace while in Atlanta for the film premier: Clark Gable, accompanied by his wife, Carole Lombard; Vivien Leigh and her soon-to-be husband, Sir Laurence Olivier; Ann Rutherford; Olivia de Havilland; and Mr. and Mrs. David O. Selznick.

The outrageously Parisian Grand Ballroom of the Georgian Terrace was the location for the December 14, 1939 *Gone with the Wind* premiere gala. All the stars were there—except black actresses, Hattie McDaniel, who scored an Acade-my Award for her role as Mammy; and Butterfly McQueen, who played Prissy. By virtue of Jim Crow, they were not welcome at the Ball. Nine-year-old Martin Luther King, Jr., however, was in attendance, singing in a "negro" boys choir from his father's Ebeneezer Baptist Church.

In that legendary ballroom, the day after I entered Atlanta, I met Joan Carey. Is it blasphemy, or mere narcissism, to say that Joan looked to me that morning like the Blessed Mother? Perhaps it was that I whispered to myself, over and over, *Mother of God*, when I first glimpsed her. Perhaps it was that day's proximity to the Feast of the Assumption that produced the vision of Joan as an iconographic hologram—blue, then pink, and clearly nimbused. By God, the South had put a spell on me.

Joan and I had been randomly seated next to each other at breakfast. A VISTA official welcomed us, then we launched into the perfunctory round-robin of introducing ourselves and where we hailed from. Joan, an Atlanta native—Tucker, Georgia, to be precise—took some umbrage at the fact she was a minority in her own hometown. The vast majority of new VISTA recruits were from the Northeast. *Yankees.* Joan wielded the word like an epithet. I was puzzled. She had equated all Northerners with the stereotypical Big Appler, a kind of mutant engendered by breeding Ratso Rizzo, played by Dustin Hoffman in *Midnight Cowboy*, with Joan Rivers–though, with some shame, I must confide that I had overheard fellow *Yankees*, in nasal Northeast yammers, remark condescendingly on the Southland's way of talking, and bellyaching over its tragic lack of bagels.

Suddenly self-conscious, I didn't defend myself. We're all stuck with our stereotypes. Besides, I wanted to watch Joan. She had about her an angularity, elasticity. Her limbs were long, lithe. As if triple-jointed, she had a way of curling her legs beneath herself and around things. I had recently developed a sincere attraction for women with freckles—not the blazing international orange mottle that smeared in the sun, but rather the more discreet auburn ellipses like Joan's that struck me as exotic, seductive, even occult. She had long shiny brown hair. Beautiful Atlantic blue, twinkling eyes, eyebrows that arched when she was amused. Barefoot—her sandals beneath the table. Her accent: soft E's were soft I's. A pen was a *pin*. On was *own*. Can't was *caint*. She said *y'all* and *kin* and *reckon*. Fascinating. Beyond adorable. Occasionally, she glanced in my direction and smiled.

I had heard of grits—mainly in books and, again, I'm embarrassed to confess, on *The Beverly Hillbillies*, a show, I should also confess, I really loved. But I had never seen grits. I allowed the sound of the word to guide my imagination. I expected something more akin to *grit*, something with crunch and decidedly darker than the soupy white puddle that arrived, alongside my eggs and bacon, when my breakfast was delivered. Confusion must have registered on my face.

"Grits," Joan prompted. "A little butter and salt. Some people like pepper too. Like this." She demonstrated and I mimicked her. I liked my grits, but not as much as listening to her. "And please don't say they remind you of Cream of Wheat. Yankees don't know any better but to put sugar in them. Restaurant grits aren't very good. The best are homemade." I stared at her as I listened. "What are you staring at?" she inquired.

I parried by asking her to have dinner with me.

"No," she said; then she said, "Yes." She had been a bit "ticked," as she put it. Just the night before, someone had tried to steal her car, a 1966 Ford Fairlane, from the hotel parking lot. "Probably a Yankee." Then she smiled.

Days blew by in a welter of meetings. VISTA had initiatives all over the Southeast: not just in prisons, but in daycares, housing projects, Planned Parenthood, women's clinics, drug and alcohol rehab centers. We listened to endless testimony from veteran VISTAs, just in from the bush, who assured us that our lives were about to radically change. We heard again and again the terms "resource mobilization" and "crisis intervention."

Our VISTA boss was Jim Plumley, a 26 year old, bearded, free-wheeling guy from South Philly who hadn't quite gotten over the Philadelphia Phillies' pennant collapse of Aristotelian proportions back in 1964. Jim was as allusive as Mark Twain and about as witty. He talked incessantly about TastyKakes, Genesee Cream Ale, and the splendor of cheese steaks and cheese cake at Ponzio's Diner in Jersey's Cherry Hill. He lived in Charlotte, worked for North Carolina's Department of Correction as a Program Director, and referred to all things prison exclusively as "the chain gang." He informed us we'd be headed to the DOC's South Piedmont Area, comprised of eleven counties, more or less in south central North Carolina, bordering South Carolina—to do what, it wasn't clear, but he instantly recruited me to play for the prison staff's basketball and softball teams.

The only other male assigned to our project was a mellow Cuban guy, my age—Ben Valdes. He too was from Georgia, Marietta, and a recent graduate of Mercer University. Tall and skinny, a big head of black hair and a scrawny black mustache—Freddie Prinze with an afro. Ben's dad, a minister, was still in Havana, locked in one of Castro's jails. We took to each other instantly. Since we'd both be working in tandem at two prisons—in Huntersville, just north of Charlotte, in Mecklenburg County; and at Mount Pleasant (what a disarming name for a prison) in a neighboring county—we decided to score a place together in Charlotte.

Joan teamed with Judy, a Jewish woman from New Jersey, with a huge kinky weir of chestnut hair. Both assigned to a unit for youthful offenders in Dallas, NC, they were going to find a place together in Gastonia, a rough little mill town the inmates dubbed "Little Chicago," with purportedly the highest murder rate per capita in the U.S. While Joan's southern pedigree remained for me a fetching anomaly, I had Judy thoroughly pegged. She was going to be trouble. She had arrived in Atlanta with her hometown boyfriend, Harry, also a new VISTA recruit. He was headed for an Alabama project and seemed not the least fretful over the separation. Judy, on the other hand, wept conspicuously over jugs of Gallo Burgundy at Harry's impending departure and their doomed love.

In the minimal spare time afforded me while not in training sessions, I read, wrote letters back home, and wandered Atlanta. Riding the Hilton Towers elevator that crawled exposed along the outside of the skyscraper up into the clouds blew my mind. Birds fluttered about the Omni lobby. I bought an *X-Men* comic book. I talked a number of times to my parents. My mother inquired repeatedly, with a note of expectant cynicism, if I liked "it," as if I might confess the folly of leaving home and point my black bug north for Mellon Street where I belonged. In truth, I didn't feel like I had left home in any determined way. I had signed onto VISTA for one year. What I'd do beyond that, I hadn't contemplated. I guess I figured, simply by default, I'd return to Pittsburgh. My contact with Joan was confined in the main to my surreptitious mooning over her during meetings.

The Turf of Hankering

In the throes of all the mingling, one of the VISTA bosses from another project approached me. Exquisitely tailored, what my mother, a seamstress, would term *fit to kill*. Beautiful white shirt, charcoal seersucker suit, splendid necktie. Handsome, coiffed beard. I liked him right away. His name was Jac. Like Jack, but no K. He ran a project on the North Carolina coast at Carolina Beach. He asked me if I wanted to jump projects, forget about prison and come to work at the beach for him as a building inspector.

Mad about the seaside—the Beat beach life my precursors had enjoyed in previous decades at Big Sur and North Beach— I had vowed I'd someday live at the ocean. I told Jac I didn't know a thing about inspecting buildings.

"What do you know about prisons?" he countered. The project would supply me with a Jeep.

Jac invited me out for a drink at The Pleasant Peasant, a suspect name now, looking back on it. But then—molting, as I was, by the minute into what would be the next grand phase of my life—the name struck me merely as cool, a true rhyme, though a joint, with such a name, that would never have made it in Pittsburgh. A peasant, in my neighborhood, was some-thing very different than on Atlanta's Peachtree Street. Atlanta seemed like that: more of everything, exponential. A kind of seductive grandiosity. Atlanta was drunk. Maybe it was hung over.

The name of the bar didn't matter to me. I had left home to see what might happen if I left home. Jac was what my mother called an operator. I knew that the second I laid eyes on him, and was unphased by it. I didn't care about that either. I had read a load of books. I was obsessing about that promised Jeep and the Atlantic Ocean and my rarified life in a little fishing shack on the sunset flank of a sand-spit where I'd write my unforgettable debut bildungsroman in 21 days on one big contiguous roll of magic paper.

Jac and I sat in at a sun-washed table with a sparkling white cloth and glinting cutlery and drank Amaretto and orange juice, a drink I had never heard of. Smooth, funny as heck, Jac paid for everything. Once you acquired your VISTA papers, your pauper status was immediately recognized in the organization. After a second round of drinks, we walked further up Peachtree to the International House of Pancakes, another first for me, for hot fudge cake. Things, in Jac's lexicon, were *posh* and *deluxe*. He assured me we'd make quite a team. I saw myself throttling the Jeep, top down, through the dunes, the Atlantic applauding me.

Joan and I had dinner at Salvatore's, next door to the hotel. I knew half a dozen Salvatores from my neighborhood. The food was mediocre, but everything else was just right. We talked in the insatiable vein of a young man and woman who want to be nowhere else but with each other. I couldn't stop staring at her—bathed again in the beatific blue light that mantels our Lady when she miraculously appears, and wearing a clairvoyant blouse, with tiny white buttons, the exact color of Mary's blue cloak.

Joan had a femininity I had never noticed in another woman—she had sensationally exquisite hands—yet she packed a .22 pistol and her own set of tools. There was the '66 two-door Ford Fairlane, with its brazen red interior. She liked to camp along the Broad River, in Clarke County outside Athens, Georgia, with her dog, Piggy Bear, a fourteen pound long-legged prognathous dervish with velvety ears, a teased mohair pelt, and metronomic tail the size of a half-smoked stogie. Half bulldog, half French poodle, son of Spud and Croquette, he ate charcoal and cigarette butts and was insanely, possessively, in love with Joan and murderously jealous. Fugitive from a fairy tale, he waited for that one foretold kiss from Princess Joan that would turn him into the handsome prince he knew himself to be—though if kisses from her could've worked that magic, he would have been a prince a million times over.

Joan had three brothers, roughly my age. They had mustaches and drove Lincoln Continentals. Along with her mother, they had been opposed to her going to VISTA. She had just graduated Magna Cum Laude from the University of Georgia with a degree in Education, after leaving high school a year early—her dream was to teach kindergarten (I swooned)—and they couldn't fathom why she would trek off to another state to willingly embrace poverty and work among criminals for no wage at all—which precisely described my parents' confusion over my decision to join VISTA.

She had grown up in Indian Creek Baptist Church and went to church on Wednesday evenings and twice on Sundays. She referred to her church's minister as *Preacher*. Her grandmothers were *Granny*. She rattled off verbatim encyclopedic lore about her home state: that Stone Mountain, the South's Mount Rushmore, carved with the faces of Jefferson Davis, Stonewall Jackson, and Robert E. Lee, is "the largest exposed granite monolith in the world"; that Button Gwinnett, for whom the county of Gwinnett, a colossal suburb of Atlanta, was named, was the second statesman to sign the Declaration of Independence.

She hated cheese, ate candy for breakfast, favored Chantilly perfume, and played piano. Her middle name was Marie—my sister's name, my mother's name, my father's mother's name.

Her paternal grandfather, Mano Carey—my grandfathers' Christian names were Paolo and Luigi—had been boyhood friends in Royston, Georgia with Ty Cobb.

When Joan was a little girl, there had been a laundromat, just across from the Dairy Queen, in downtown Tucker. On the floor above, the Ku Klux Klan, in their white robes and imbecilic hats, had gathered. There were summer nights when she gazed beyond her vast backyard, through the woods, and made out a cross burning in Venable's Field.

She was only twenty years old when I met her. Her father had died 16 days before.

How does one so instantly become an intimate, a confidante, of another? Two strangers so culturally and geographically distant? What cosmic dynamic is at play? The delicacy, the risk, the unlikelihood? Despite inevitable embarrassment, I wish I had a transcript of the various leaps in conversation that so instantly bonded us. I don't remember a particular pivot, any sleight of hand I employed, or Joan demurring whatsoever. We were completely happy, even ecstatic, that night in Salvatore's in the amnesty of each other's company, realizing our lives had suddenly changed in ways we had yet to imagine. What, I wonder, might I have shared with her? I would have told her, I'm certain, about the kinds of things she had told me: family, religion, education, dreams, aspirations. I'll bet I told her how viciously the nuns had treated me; that always fetched the kind of sympathy I craved from women. I might have even confided that I wanted to be a writer. Women adore sensitive men (Jimmy Carter, a Geor-gian, was running for president).

Somehow, during dinner, I got to talking to the maitre d', an Italian guy. During World War II he had been a Marine recruiter in East Liberty, the very neighborhood I grew up in. He was pretty sure he knew my mother and her brothers and sisters.

So what was going on? I was in the deep South, but I kept running into people from home—as if to remind me of who I was. I gazed over a candle at a Georgia woman who referred to me as a *Yankee,* and with whom—it was obvious to me even though I had only known her twelve hours—I had fallen in love. I was suddenly aware of a number of things: that I was a *Yankee,* a term that in the North designates a professional base-ball player, but in the South is a kind of slur; that a *Yankee* in that *place,* the South, was thoroughly undesirable; that while I was physically in the South, I was psychically rooted in another *place,* Pittsburgh, that now existed only in my imagination, yet which I had lugged with me (how else could one explain all those Pittsburghers I kept running into?); that I had come under the sway of a woman, Joan Carey; that my consciousness, as to my own place, and how it related to my identity, had already begun revising itself. I was, before my very own eyes, metamorphosing.

Eudora Welty, in her essay, *Place in Fiction,* says of the writer: "Place is where he has his roots, place is where he stands; in his experience out of which he writes, it provides the base of reference; in his work, the point of view."

Place has always been for me two places: the moment in which, with my feet on a particular turf, I'm breathing; and also that other life I've banked like a sheltered account in

Pittsburgh. Yet, too, there is the turf of longing—or should I say *hankering*—the abstract we choose to call home: where one hangs one's hat; where the heart is; where, as Robert Frost writes, "[W]hen you have to go there, / They have to take you in."

Hadn't Joan said *homemade* was best? Her home was in the South. Yet it conjured for her, as did my home for me, all those clichés about the "clean, well-lighted place," a sanctuary of goodness, spirituality, psychic cosmos, optimism, nostalgia. In all likelihood, *home* is an illusion, though nonetheless powerful for being so. One keeps returning to it—even when turning away from it—for the nourishment that *place*, overburdened with mythos and perhaps entirely imagined, can alone supply. Never mind the pain. "Memory," as James Joyce said, "is unreliable." Point of view thrives in the marrow of subjectivity.

My last night in Atlanta, Joan and I were out cruising in her big white Fairlane when she surprised me with the fact that we were going to have dinner with her mother, back in Tucker, in the house on Idlewood Road, the only one she had ever lived in before departing for college.

At the time, I was clothed in a T-shirt, ratty pair of jeans, and hadn't shaved in two or three days. Knowing the universal appeal of a clean-shaven face and first impressions—and here I was projecting accurately, I might add, onto Joan's mother a predilection of my own mother's—I insisted she stop at a convenience store so I could buy shaving gear. In an adjacent besotted gas station bathroom, equipped with only cold water, I lathered my face with Tahitian fruit foam and hacked away. I was about to enter my first authentic Southern home.

Joan referred to her mom not as *my mother*, but exclusively *Mother*; and she was decidedly up front, as though preparing me, that her mother, a Bible-believing Christian, a dyed-in-the-wool Southern Baptist, was pretty serious about her religion. Not only did she not believe in smoking, drinking, dancing and gambling—things I had judicious affection for—but she regarded them sins. Her name was Rowena, actually Hattie Rowena. Her maiden name was Wikle, and she was born in Anniston, Alabama. At age 17, she had married Joan's father, Darren Lee Carey (nicknamed Ike), recently returned from World War II. At some point they divorced, remarried, and divorced again. Not only had I never heard of remarrying someone you'd divorced, but I was unaware such a thing was permitted. Joan's mother had raised four children on her own, often working two, sometimes three, jobs to keep her children clothed, fed, warm and all together under one roof. She planted and tended a huge garden and cut her acre and a half of grass on a riding mower. She worked for Scott Foresman Publishing as an Accounts Manager.

By my lights, Tucker, fifteen miles northeast of Atlanta, was way out in the country. Idlewood was an eerily quiet wide road, its smattering of houses spaced far apart, rural mailboxes on posts in front of each. Very few people. The house itself was a small ranch-style, similar to those in working class suburbs like Penn Hills, in Pittsburgh, where Patricia had grown up— so very different than the row houses and apartments on skinny one-way streets in my bustling neighborhood. Joan parked beneath the carport at the edge of her vast backyard. We entered the house through the kitchen. I was instantly put at ease by the fabulous smells. Joan had bragged about her mother's cooking.

The evening I met Mrs. Carey, she was 47, born in 1929, the year of The Crash, the same year Dr. King was born. Over her dress, she wore an apron. Her hands and wrists were dusted with flour. She had the same blue eyes as Joan, deeply set in the same quizzical brow, but there was about her a studied perplexity, as if at every moment she was appraising the situation—or, in this case, suspiciously sizing up the Italian-Catholic-Yankee from Pittsburgh who had just barged through her back door with her only daughter with whom, by this time, nearly five days, he was earnestly flinging. As Joan introduced us, my eyes fell upon one of the refrigerator magnets: *This is the first day of the rest of your life.* On the counter presided a black leather-bound Bible, dog-eared, annotated, and foxed. Out of it flowed notes in lovely penmanship, Mrs. Carey's initials gold-stamped in its lower right corner.

As everyone knows, it is around the dinner table, in close proximity to the kitchen, that ethnocentricity, in whatever guise, is hatched. I found myself seated at a table laden with *homemade* food: ham, biscuits, black-eyed peas, okra (fried, mercifully), and collard greens—the last three of which I had never seen before, much less eaten.

We sat and suddenly Mrs. Carey solemnly bowed her head, closed her eyes (Protestants close their eyes when they pray), reached one hand toward Joan, and one toward me. Joan clutched her mother's hand. I took the other. Then Joan and I linked hands, so that the three of us formed a triangle of prayer. There I was, in Tucker, Georgia, holding hands with my new Southern girlfriend and her mother.

Mrs. Carey then said Grace, though she called it "the blessing" and "returning thanks." The standard Catholic Grace I grew up with, the only Grace I knew, is: *Bless us, O Lord, and these thy gifts, which we are about to receive, through thy bounty, through Christ, Our Lord. Amen.* A formulaic anthem one rattles off with the same alacrity as the *Hail Mary.* Mrs. Carey's Grace was extemporaneous. It started with "Father, we thank you" and went wherever she was moved to take it, like automatic writing, an anguished poetic improvisation. It was amazing. I kept my eyes open.

I had never in my life broken bread in the house of Protestants. Let me clarify that: *Southern Baptists.* What's more—despite being 23 years old and ostensibly educated at a solid university—it only dawned on me that night that the Baptist faith is not exclusively comprised of African-Americans. The only Baptist congregations I was aware of in Pittsburgh were black—and wild holy rollers to boot. Their churches were frequently termed *missions* and *tabernacles,* and their singing and signification tided out their bright red open doors into the avenues.

On the other hand, it seemed that Catholics, at least in the precincts I dined that night, were similarly misapprehended. I soon realized there was one thing about which Joan's mother was too apprehensive to keep silent: my Papist origins. And so it came to pass that talk, despite Joan's protests of *Mother!* fell quickly to my denominational affliction—though I stood forewarned by Joan that talk would inevitably turn in this direction. I was grilled about the Pope, Confession, Purgatory, and my relationship with Jesus, who, by this time, I expected any minute to walk in and help Himself to supper. I was polite, charming and deferential, yet unable, really, to account for all my nutty liturgy except to acknowledge it—how the heck can you explain Catholicism to a non-Catholic?—Joan the entire time chanting a remonstrance of *Mother! Mother! Mother!*

It dawned on me that Mrs. Carey's interrogation, pensive, though congenial, was rooted in a deep, near-obsessive suspicion of Northerners triggered by the legacy of the Civil War; Union invasion and occupation; the infamous carpet-baggers; ceaseless raids on the South's pristine, though rapidly dwindling, real estate; and the South's sense not of inferiority, but its sense that it is *thought* to be inferior. And there are a thousand other psychical things that I, as an outsider, can never quite comprehend. Place, like blood, remains mysterious.

Mrs. Carey *was* the South and I, a by-God Yankee, a *Blue-belly*, had marched into her home with designs on her ravishing *Belle* of a daughter. That I was an Italian Catholic did not aid the cause. At one point, Mrs. Carey proclaimed: "Y'all think we're all barefoot and pregnant." She could have been speaking Aramaic. At the time, I had no earthly idea what she meant, no context whatsoever—commentary, I'm certain, on my own provincialism.

I did, however, assure Mrs. Carey that my relationship with Jesus, albeit idiosyncratic, was on the up and up, though by the time I met her, I was a non-practicing Catholic—*lapsed* in the vocabulary of the Holy See—readying (*fixing,* as Joan might say) to imperil my immortal soul, according to church canon, through consort with her thoroughly non-Catholic daughter.

I'll admit I was a tad uncomfortable by all the pointed allusions to religion. I grew up in an orthodox Roman Catholic culture. I attended pathologically strict Catholic schools—Religion class every day—through high school. Taught by fiendish, abusive nuns in grade school, then benign, sane Christian Brothers in high school. I was an altar boy, a choir boy, Mass every morning except Saturdays (when I was forced to go to

Confession). In each bedroom of my home was a crucifix. Easter palm tucked into every drawer and closet. Rosaries, missals, medals, statues, scapulars, holy cards, and even mini holy water fonts. I made the Sign of the Cross every time I passed a (Catholic) church. My dad's Chrysler Newport had a magnetized statue of the Sacred Heart on the dashboard and a Saint Christopher icon pinned to the sun visor. He had crosses in his toolbox. Even our cellar was a reliquary. Depended from my neck that night in Tucker was my medal of Saint Joseph (the patron saint of fathers and husbands and workers), holding in his carpenter's arms the infant Prince of Peace. Engraved, in Italian, on the back of the medal, was *Dio mi protega*. God protect me.

I could hold my own on Bible lore with any Protestant. My entire life had been a devotion, often under duress, but the tradition was there, stamped into me as irrevocably as DNA. In other words, I was no neophyte when it came to religion, and I had the scars to prove it.

Where I came from, however, religion, like sexual practices, was considered intensely personal and not usually inquired about. Especially by strangers. Flannery O'Connor, a right famous Georgia Catholic, known to admix in her stories both eroticism and religion simultaneously, once quipped, "While the South is hardly Christ-centered, it is most certainly Christ-haunted." But, in defense of Mrs. Carey, she had of course by then heard from Joan that our relationship seemed to be gaining momentum; and because I represented an anomaly—Italian-Catholic-Yankee from Pittsburgh—which her maternal antennae had singled out as a potential son-in-law, it had not been in her power to refrain from asking me certain questions.

While sort of failing the personal salvation component of the test, I gained big ground by eating enormously, proving I was not just another squeamish sorry Yank who couldn't face down a belly-full of collards, peas, and okra. The ultimate art of self-ingratiation is to honor the cook.

At some point, I excused myself. To get to the bathroom, I had to walk through Mrs. Carey's bedroom. When I saw her beautiful four-poster cherry wood bed, bead and scroll work, vintage 1940s, I gasped. It was the absolute exact same bed that rested in my parents' bedroom. I had never seen its like anywhere else before. Yet there it was, in Tucker, Georgia, 750 miles from its doppelganger on Mellon Street in Pittsburgh, Pennsylvania. A wagering man, I knew those odds were a sucker bet—even a piker wouldn't have touched them with a ten foot pole—but that number had hit. Astonished, dizzy, I stared at my folks' bed. I would also discover, before the night was over, that Mrs. Carey and my mother shared the same birthday, May 31st. Gemini: twins. A few times that evening, Mrs. Carey had declared that "He doesn't close one door, but he opens another." What portal had I traipsed through?

When it was time for Joan and me to leave, the three of us at the door clasped hands again. Mrs. Carey bowed her head and launched into another improvised, impassioned benediction. Her voice broke a number of times as she prayed evangelically that the Heavenly Father guide us in our sojourn through the night and for all the years to come on this troubled planet so rife with meanness. She had sprung full-bore from the pages of Flannery O'Connor: Mrs. Chestny in "Everything That Rises Must Converge," yes, but even more so the famous Grandmother in "A Good Man Is Hard to Find"—a Pure-T, flat-out archetype.

When Mrs. Carey concluded, tears glistened in her blue eyes and rolled down her cheeks. Then she fixed Joan's blue eyes with hers and whispered, without a whit of hesitation, "I love you," whereupon Joan prayerfully responded, "I love you too." It took my breath.

I don't remember exactly what words I used that night to say goodbye to Mrs. Carey. I think we both suspected, however, that we'd be seeing a lot of each other. By then, I had informed Jac that, enticing as his offer was, I had in mind something even more poignant than a Jeep and a beach address.

The next day I climbed back into my black VW and bolted off to Charlotte, my VISTA gig at Huntersville Prison, and my first crack at writing gaudy stories about postmodern chain gang life. Quite literally, I had no idea whatsoever what was I in for. Nevertheless, in the spirit of Mrs. Carey, I took a leap of faith—she had assured me repeatedly that evening that "He provides beyond our needs"—and followed her beautiful daughter.

I was about to be handed a narrative. What could be stranger, I wondered, as I tooled up I-85 into the North Carolina Piedmont. Did I think that new territory would end up my *home*? Would that have been the *word* I used? I don't know. What I do know is that my eye and ear were already being changed by the somewhere-else Southern scapes and inflections, by the weather of a context the writer calls *place*, and everybody else calls home.

Ghost, Come Back Again

It had started to snow on our tiny, yellow cottage in Shuffletown as dusk came on and, when the call came from Patricia, there were probably six inches in our backyard—a rarity in that part of the North Carolina Piedmont. I sat on the living room's garish calico shag carpet, leaning against the baseboard heater. Phoebe Snow's *It Looks Like Snow* played on our Goodwill turntable. Joan and I had opened a bottle of red wine; we figured we were in for the night.

Patricia wanted Joan and I to drive to Boone. It was snowing like mad up there and she and her boyfriend Dave were having a party at her house on Poplar Creek Road. They had been our great friends on Oakland Avenue in Charlotte where we'd lived just before and after marrying, and we hadn't seen them since we'd all split for different precincts. Through the phone, I heard jubilation in the background. I told Patricia that we were besieged by snow ourselves and settled in. We were going to sit tight. Joan was fine with that. It made no sense to get on the road. It was nine o'clock. We were alone, happy, drinking wine in the middle of a white-out in Shuffletown.

The phone rang again. This time it was Dave. He made the same plea as Patricia, but more passionately with an inflection of challenge. Again, I heard those Appalachian State kids raising hell in the background. They were having a good time. *Where was I?* He made me feel like I was missing something. It was December of 1980. I was 27. Joan had just turned 25.

We grabbed a few things and jumped into our VW Squareback and headed north on Highway 16. I didn't consult a map. Maybe I got directions from Dave. It was snowing so hard we couldn't make out the bridge as we crossed the Catawba into Gaston County, just a mile into our journey. Mountain Island Lake stretched silver toward the chuffing stacks of the mysterious power plant on the water. Laura's Rozzelle House, last of the mythic Southern all-you-can-eat family-style manses, kept its counsel on the near bank, and Thomas Wolfe, as he often did, chanted in my head: *O lost, and by the wind grieved, ghost come back again.*

I had visited the North Carolina mountains for the first time before we married. Joan and I, then living in Charlotte, travelled west on Independence Boulevard until it became a dizzying series of two-lane switchbacks. By the time we fetched Asheville, we were sick with vertigo, and the city seemed nothing like Scott and Zelda's Shangri-La. Downtown Asheville, in 1976, was dank and haggard. Like one of the little steel towns dotting the banks of the three big rivers that swept out of my hometown Pittsburgh. I liked Asheville very much. Joan and I walked among clouds that sailed like dirigibles across the sky, their shadows falling across the face of the bluish mountains. I had never stood at such altitude.

I had only heard of Thomas Wolfe. I owned a copy of *You Can't Go Home Again* (if nothing else, its title seemed apropos of a cruel inevitability), a Signet paperback that sold new for 95 cents, ten years before in 1966, though the great big novel first appeared in 1940. I had planned to read it one day but never had. In fact, I managed to earn a Master's Degree in English Literature from the University of Pittsburgh without ever reading a word by Thomas Wolfe. In all likelihood, back then,

I had conflated Thomas Wolfe with Tom Wolfe, the white linen-suited new journalist, who wrote *The Electric Kool-Aid Acid Test*.

That weekend, as Joan and I strolled Asheville, we came upon Old Kentucky Home (called Dixieland in Wolfe's first novel, *Look Homeward, Angel*). It had been Thomas Wolfe's boyhood home, a 29 room Queen Anne boarding house—turrets and gables and porches mitered into the upper stories—painted white, built in 1883, and ramrodded by his imperious mother, Julia Wolfe. It had been kept over the years as a literary shrine to the memory of Wolfe.

Joan swooned indiscriminately over all things educational—she had been trained as a teacher at the University of Georgia—the more antique the better. Touring someone's home did not interest me. But I would have done anything to please her, not to mention that I wished to come off as urbane. Plus, I wanted to be a writer—had indeed begun composing my first stories in our cramped attic garret in Charlotte we lived in at the time—and I was well aware that Wolfe had been a famous one. Something extraordinary must have happened to hasten his genius in those sprawling plaster rooms he had begun living in at age 6, before departing in 1916 to matriculate at the state university in Chapel Hill.

We paid to get in, then ambled the museum-like rooms, decked in the period livery and accoutrement of Wolfe's era. The house had the funereal, mausoleum aura of the Pompei ruins—as if the family had moments before been spirited away, but left everything in pristine shape for expected company, half a century later. The rooms I entered had no real significance for me. Again, I hadn't read a solitary syllable Wolfe had penned.

Joan enjoyed the house for its curios and furniture, its palpable witness of the vanished *noblesse oblige* of mythic Southern lore. She hailed from *Gone with the Wind* country, Atlanta, and she wore back then, when I first met her, a mantle of fierce love of everything south of the Mason-Dixon, the further south the better. I heard her once say that North Carolina was getting a little too far north. She was still in her Yankee-loathing phase, and her abiding suspicion of us was unrelenting. Somehow I had earned clemency. I was a Yankee, she'd grudgingly admit, but not a damn Yankee.

As I wandered the rooms, I had no idea that I was laying eyes on W.O. Wolfe's actual stone cutter's tools, that the grand fireplace I glanced at was where W.O. and then his counterpart from *Look Homeward, Angel*, Oliver Gant, doused the laid hearth in kerosene of a morning, and with a single match set off a blaze like a rocket to warm his children. Nor the very china and flatware, the tureens, and pitchers Julia Wolfe and then her fictional doppelgänger, Eliza Gant, set before her strange boarders. The room, the very bed, where Benjamin Harrison Wolfe, Thomas's brother, would die in and then die in again, still Ben, his name not changed in the fiction, in *Look Homeward, Angel*. It was all there, spread before me; I just wasn't aware of its significance.

Then I crossed the threshold of a bedroom, upstairs, and in an opened closet hung a massive camel-hair topcoat, swaying almost imperceptibly in whatever breath suspired throughout that house. Beneath it on the floor sat a pair of enormous plain brown oxfords, the laces untied as if Wolfe had just stepped out of them. On a table in the middle of the room brooded a solemn black typewriter—an antique Remington or Olivetti, the name flourished in gold above the tiered keyboard. Light sluiced through the white sheer curtains. The very last of it burnishing that coat and shoes, flashing off the gilt keys of the typewriter.

It was the end of the day—beatified with all the ineffability with which Wolfe wrote. I stood in that room with the woman I loved—she really believed that someday I'd be a writer—and something occurred that my Catholic disposition, even now, latches onto as the gift of grace. I found myself miraculously transformed into a Thomas Wolfe fanatic, evangelized, I swear, by his topcoat and shoes. Nothing more poignant, nor memorable. And, most astonishing of all, I had never read a word he'd written.

That deficit, however, was quickly remedied. I like to think I rushed out of Old Kentucky Home to the nearest bookstore, aglow like Paul after he was knocked from his horse on the road to Damascus, and purchased everything authored by Wolfe they carried. What I do know is that I hurtled into a pathological and exhaustive study of Thomas Wolfe. Appropriately, I launched first into *Look Homeward, Angel* and was "touched by that dark miracle of chance which makes new magic in a dusty world." I adored the book. Then onto *Of Time and the River;* and the Wolfe biography by Elizabeth Nowell, Wolfe's literary agent; and *The Letters of Thomas Wolfe,* edited by Nowell. I ripped through *The Window of Memory,* by Richard Kennedy; *The Mountains,* edited by Pat Ryan, a book containing Wolfe's Plays; the biographies *Aline* by Carole Klein, about Wolfe's lover, Aline Bernstein; and A. Scott Berg's wonderful *Max Perkins: Editor of Genius.* I read *Thomas Wolfe and His Family*, by Mable Wolfe Wheaton (Wolfe's sister, portrayed as Helen in *Look Homeward, Angel*), with LeGette Blythe. I even tackled *Thomas Wolfe: The Critical*

Reception, edited by Paschal Reeves, a compendium of reviews, scholarly abstracts and précis—the kinds of writing that in my former life I had carefully steered clear of because of how tawdry and boring I found them. Joan and I visited Wolfe's grave at Riverside Cemetery. I had more or less lost my mind.

By the time we moved out of Charlotte to Shuffletown, I had pussel-gutted myself on Thomas Wolfe. There, in the yellow cottage, I had a little study and, at a wooden table I had nailed together myself, I began my first novel, an unapologetically swooning bildungsroman in homage to Wolfe that I called, Good God, in the overwrought spirit of Wolfe, *Perhaps, by Love Bequeathed.* It was, of course, about growing up in Pittsburgh, the city lately called the Paris of Appalachia. Perhaps some muse of my homeland's geography, its hills, coal barges and steel, its hardheaded devotion to grime and toil and hardscrabble had infiltrated my consciousness, my soul, as I set out to mimic Thomas Wolfe. He had wanted to say everything: in a never-before-apprehended mad poetic epistemological rant, sheer unbridled passion, the more the better—and so did I, not unlike, I'm sure other, unwashed writers just starting out.

I worked my book every day in joy and certainty—some of the most inspired and glorious writing I've ever bent my head over. I'll always be grateful for those days there in Shuffletown, basking in the unlikely and utter dazzle that I was the brilliant heir apparent to Wolfe. Had I been attached to cigarettes, I would have chain-smoked. Had I been tall enough, I would have stood and used the top of our refrigerator to write on—as Wolfe had done. Instead I sat and wrote everything out longhand in tiny immaculate cursive on a legal pad, then typed the day's yield on my old Underwood, using carbon paper to produce a second copy.

I was writing my own family saga, filled with melodrama and tenderness and oozing with heartbreaking, flowery sentimentality, channeling the gargantuan Wolfe—and he never let me down. I let it all go in that over-the-top frenzy of words he was so famous for: three-four adjectives for every one. Pages filled in a weir of impenetrable, impressionistic language that I told myself made sense. Words and more words—that I counted over and over. Output was everything. Somewhere I had read that Wolfe, after a feast at Cherio's, his favorite restaurant, lumbered through Manhattan on one of his legendary interminable treks muttering a litany of "I wrote ten thousand words today, I wrote ten thousand words today."

Like Wolfe, I drank indecent amounts of coffee as I wrote. Cup after cup, pot after pot, until I was so deranged with caffeine I'd barge out our front door and yawp barbarically at the crows in the pine trees ringing the cottage and they'd yawp back in affirmation. I refused food until nightfall, then fell asleep dreaming about what I'd written that day, what I'd write the next. I was certain that what I scribed at that table was good, damn good, that it would guarantee my fame as a writer, that when I sat in that room I was in the grip of something wholly fire-breathing original. The Muse had its claws lodged in my capacious heart. There's a good chance I was never happier.

That night we left Shuffletown for my second trip to the North Carolina mountains, this time to Boone, in Watauga County, I was very much under the spell of Thomas Wolfe. Raw experience was what I was after, and the caprice that night in the blizzard proved worth it. Joan and I would only realize a day later on our return home when we could actually see the skinny winding roads hanging over the escarpments we'd travelled to get there, how insane we'd been to attempt the journey in the first place.

Somehow we made it up the mountain into Boone. I inched up Poplar Creek Road, on the fringe of Appalachian's campus, peering into the driving snow for our friend's house, when at us charged a brigade of wild students on skis down the middle of the road to welcome us, the heroic wayfarers we fancied ourselves.

Later that night, after much good cheer and revelry, and the onset of desperate hunger, the most miraculous event of the evening occurred. Patricia picked up the phone for take-out—Joan and I gasped in incredulity—and in short order a Jeep commandeered by an intrepid grinning kid grinded up with a sack of meatball sandwiches from Sollecito's, an Italian joint that delivered in blizzards at 3 a.m. *Holy God*, I thought, standing in the middle of the road in a foot and a half of snow eating the indescribably delicious sandwich, *I want to live here*.

I never dreamed that, twenty-two years later, I would land a job teaching creative writing at Appalachian State University, that those inscrutable amazing mountains that shrouded my future that snowy night long ago would become my beloved home.

Of course, my Thomas Wolfe novel was no good, but it took a little while before that fact hit me. I don't apologize for it not being good. It's no secret that one has to write poorly before writing well. Nevertheless, that realization came with true regret, and reluctantly I scrapped my book. Not long after, I lost traction with Wolfe as well, and never made it all the way through *The Web and the Rock*. I still haven't read *You Can't Go Home Again*—though I'll always love Wolfe and will be forever grateful to him, to his overcoat and shoes, to whatever happened to me the day I traipsed into Old Kentucky Home. I'm willing to call it mystical. It made me want to write a book every day, to fill my own steamer trunk with stained and tattered foolscap.

Thinking Big Budget:
Twenty-Five Bucks and Two Cans of Bud

Nearly a year after Steven Spielberg and Moon Song Productions had finished filming *The Color Purple*, in 1985, on Harry and Betty Huntley's farm, the anonymous North Carolina county of Anson—without a functioning movie theatre in its 533 square miles—basks in its dubious proximity to Hollywood. Its citizens still regale themselves in purple, have each seen numerous times the famous film—which features their flesh and blood neighbors right up there on the big screen—and are quick to point out that only a mere four minutes of footage shot in neighboring Union County, in the town of Marshville, made it into the final product.

Not only does Anson County regard itself as synonymous with *The Color Purple*, but in truth has come to believe it engendered it. The international publicity and the five million dollars invested into the area as a result of Spielberg's presence exulted the poor little county, in the middle of the state, bordering Chesterfield County, South Carolina. It will never be the same.

The capstone of the *The Color Purple* extravaganza was The Anson County Academy Awards. Perhaps anticipating being shut out on Academy Awards night, Anson County held at its country club *The Anson Academy Awards*. In a reverent satire of the ceremony, it awarded *The Color Purple* Oscars in all the traditional categories. The only disappointment was that Spielberg himself, who had been formally invited, and whom the diehards felt sure would in Pentecostal fashion appear, did not show. Nevertheless, *The Color Purple* was officially commended to legend.

During the same month of *The Anson Academy Awards*, March of 1986, Detroit-based Renaissance Motion Pictures rather quietly appeared in Anson County and made known its plans to shoot *Evil Dead II*, a portion of which would be filmed, like its famous predecessor, *The Color Purple*, on Huntley farm land.

Harry Huntley, evangelized by *The Color Purple*, often goes about his farm chores listening with tears in his eyes to Quincey Jones' soundtrack of the film. When asked what a cattle man is doing fooling around with the motion picture industry, he replies, "Cows, hell; we're in the movie business."

It is July 29, 1986. It has been a hellish summer. Anson corn hangs brown, dead and brittle in its traces. Poultry farmers haul trucks of dead chickens and turkeys to the landfill. The tallow-colored sun, bigger than the sky, ravens the bled land. Drought-stricken farmers murder themselves. The county waits for the Federal government to declare it a disaster area.

Nowhere does disaster seem more imminent than the eastern brink of Anson, known as the Ballast Pits. A little known, yet cherished, fact is that this area of the county produces a grade of the planet's finest gravel. The price for this is an otherworldly landscape: dynamited, gouged and dredged for its granite and quartzite, then left to its own desolation. A landscape congenial only to pit vipers, dirt bikes, deranged lovers, and B-grade horror films.

It is at the edge of just such a scape I stand, with about two dozen others, as well as a contingent of horsemen and horsewomen, awaiting my crack at wardrobe. I have landed, through neither fault nor talent, a day's work as an extra in *Evil Dead II*.

Evil Dead II, as one might surmise from its title, is a spinoff of its forerunner, *The Evil Dead*, a graduate film project at Michigan State University. *The Evil Dead's* shoestring history is murky, but somehow it made it to the 1982 Cannes Film Festival where horror impresario, Stephen King, endorsed it as "The most ferociously original horror film ..." Inexplicably it became a cult classic, creating at least enough interest to prompt its Dino DeLaurentiis-backed sequel.

Evil Dead II is pure pastiche: a series of sight gags, malapropisms, idiotic one-liners, bone, gore, and viscera trumped up to the point of absurdity. *The New York Times* dubbed it "one of the goofiest, goriest movies this side of the grave."

Thus, for their obvious spoofing of the *Elm Street-Halloween*-teen-jeopardy-pajama-party-massacre-genre, *Evil Dead II* can be credited with the kind of stylized, seemingly empty-headed narrative that became de rigeur for that pedigree. It's all a big joke. The decidedly fluid plot as well: Ash, played by Bruce Campbell, a young actor blessed with Mel Gibson looks and a truly inspired range of screams and apoplexies, stumbles onto the ubiquitous *Book of the Dead*, which the film's prologue discloses "serves as a passageway to the evil world beyond." He is promptly sucked into a kaleidoscopic wind tunnel that eventually drops him into the 14th century (of Black Plague fame)—in this case, the Anson County Ballast Pits, just down the road from Gum Springs Baptist Church—during which time, film-goers learn, the *Book of the Dead* originally disappeared. Ash, perhaps because of the sawed-off shotgun he brandishes in one hand and the chainsaw he wears prosthetically in place of the other, lopped off earlier in the film, is hailed as the Messiah by a rag-tag band of knights in army surplus armor. This is where I come in.

I'm being fitted for my armor. Wardrobe is a large, open mortuary tent staked to the edge of a precipice. It is mid-morning. The sun blurs over the parapets of Kondar, a "forced perspective miniature" castle facade of plywood and two-by-fours. Already the temperature is but two digits from one hundred. The wardrobe guy, a lank, snippy Michigander, can't stand it. He wears an artfully knotted hanky on his head; his sunglasses hook to a neck chain. He "can't believe the heat." He "can't believe anybody lives here." What he "wouldn't do for a frozen Margarita."

We ignore him, pretend we relish the heat, guffaw a bit, and say things like: "Hot. This ain't nothin'. Wait till August." All of the armor, what there is of it, is plastic; but there are some authentic spears and swords. Though disillusioned by the phony armor, I'm reconciled to it; but I'm hell-bent on having a real sword. I reach into the bin and pull out a gleaming, heavy-hilted, yard-long broadsword. My compatriots do likewise.

"No. No," bleats the wardrobe guy. His three young women assistants giggle. "Not that one. Not those." But again we ignore him. Those extras who come after us will get plastic swords; and some of them, too late even for plastic armor, will be wrapped—no kidding—in aluminum foil. Before we don our armor, the three young women wrap us crudely in muslin—locally purchased, I might add—to simulate, I suppose, medieval jerkins which are then secured with twine, also purchased locally. Thus arrayed, we stand around, goofing and mugging, indulge in a bit of swordplay and wait to be called upon.

I have been apprised of the splendors of working as one of Stephen's extras (Spielberg insisted they call him Stephen) in *The Color Purple:* secret locations; gorgeous vintage clothing; Perrier and string quartets during breaks; elegant catered lunches of Veal Oscar, truffles, Fettucine Alfredo, Dom Perig-non; hobnobbing with the likes of Danny Glover, Whoopi Goldberg, Oprah Winfrey, Rae Dawn Chong, and Alice Walker.

Standing at the edge of the abandoned red crater, gazing at a forlorn scape with little resemblance to what I've imagined of making movies, and baking in my embarrassing petroleum armor, I am disappointed. But then I hear the hopeful cry: "Lunch." Down at the chow tent, smoke rises over what must be the caterers' salvers.

When I get to a place in the chow line where I can actually see the silver vat blobbed with glutinous pork barbeque, canopied with big black flies, I decide to skip lunch. It is now 103 degrees. Beneath the sauna of my armor, I am drenched. I grab one of the small bags of chips and a cup of water, squat in a corner of the tent; and watch a stunt man drive a big old four-door blue Buick off a hundred foot cliff, then clamber out of the wreck and hike back up the cliff to dine.

Finally, at about two o'clock, we are marched into the bowels of the ballast pit and introduced to director, Sam Raimi (who will go on to direct films like *The Quick and the Dead, For Love of the Game* and the *Spider-Man* movies). Raimi's a regular working-class-looking guy, twenty-six, from Chicago. He wears shorts, work boots, a sweat-soaked sleeveless T-shirt and shades. He barks directions with a bullhorn and has a sense of humor. His mantra is "Think big budget." Everything about him eschews Hollywood.

We extras, atitter at this brush with immortality, are stationed in columns on either side of a miniature railroad track upon which is mounted a camera, used to gradually back off a shot of a promontory on which star, Bruce Campbell (Ash), preens. Sporting chainsaw and shotgun, and showing all the wear and tear of a long night with demons and a culminating seven hundred year trip through time, he bellows "No," over and over, contorting his face into masks, respectively, of incredulity, terror, amnesia. High above him, on the rim of the pit, loom the fake ramparts of Kondar. The camera, on its track, rolls away from him. Our jobs are to kneel, two by two, face Campbell, raise our swords and shout "Hail," as the camera rides past us. Raimi calls for multiple takes, exhorting us to "Think big budget." When we finally get it right, he yells, "It's a wrap. Put it in the can"—indulging in such jargon, I'm sure, for our benefit. A little fringe that makes being an extra all worthwhile.

One last scene. "Think big budget," Raimi urges with a smile, then beckons to the horse-folk. In the spirit of John Ford, they careen down the cliff-side, raining even more grit into the already unbreathable air. According to a thermometer one of the grips carries, it is 121 degrees on the pit floor. Three people have keeled over from dehydration and are hauled to the shade of the chow tent.

Raimi singles out a dozen infantrymen, including me. We are situated between two swarms of mounted knights and made to run, shrieking and waving our weapons, across the pit bottom. The trick, of course, is to run fast enough not to get run over by the riders galloping behind us, but not so fast as to get one's head taken off by those in front of us. The horses are spooked. They rear out on their riders, who obviously have trouble controlling them.

I'm in a dead sprint and somewhat alarmed. Each time I yell, over the pounding horses, my mouth fills with dust. I can't get a decent breath. The sweat and dirt running into my eyes, and the fact that my helmet visor won't stay up, virtually blind me. I'm also wearing a pair of faux, flopping armored leggings which make it near impossible to run with the velocity necessary to keep from being trampled. My mates flail around me. My authentic sword grows heavier and heavier.

Again we do take after take until finally Raimi bullhorns, "It's a wrap," and we fall over like medieval Keystone Cops. This scene, the one I am most proud of, will never make it into the movie. We are finished.

For Anson County, it's just another day of making movies. For me: twenty-five dollars cash money and two cans of Budweiser from the fifty-five gallon stash trucked in to placate the brutalized extras. But the ultimate rewards go well beyond this. My picture, visor up, sunglasses on, toothpick between teeth, will be displayed prominently on the front page of *The Monroe Enquirer-Journal*. So what if they identify me by another's name? And, when I finally rent *Evil Dead II*, some six years after my part in it, I am elated to discover the split-second shot of a right arm, unmistakably mine, in the lower left corner of the film frame, hoisting a sword in benediction to the agonized Ash.

Irony

I'm at the podium. Spread in front of me, in a hall which seats, let's say, two hundred people, are about forty. Many of my poems are indecently autobiographical, and several in the book from which I'm reading are about the nuns who taught me during my first eight years of parochial school.

In embellishment of what, I'm not sure, but in between reading poems, I tell the audience a story. When I was in first grade, Sister Sarah, because there was no other way to communicate, sent messages to her fellow teachers, nuns exclusively, via children in our room. The core of her pets mainly delivered these folded notes, but in due time everyone got his chance. Everyone but I.

I had been repeatedly made aware that I was a bad boy, along with the fact that privilege, as a matter of course, was withheld from bad boys. Nevertheless, I was ravenous with envy and pined to be her chosen messenger.

One day, Sister Sarah called me to the front of the room and handed me a piece of paper folded neatly in half. Gazing at it in my hands, I made out the perfect, indecipherable penmanship swirling through the page's backsides. My task was to take the note to Sister Geralda, the principal, who also taught eighth grade, and of whom I was utterly terrified.

Sister Geralda was a relatively small woman, but she gave the impression of being iron, like a spike bent and then hammered improperly back into shape. In fact, she had a peculiar curve to her body which, like everything else, I may be imagining. It seems for the sake of caricature alone, it would be convenient, even safe, to ascribe to her a limp, a peg, perhaps a hook, some gothic prosthetic. But, truly, her head, especially, had on one side a dentedness; and in the concavity, along the temple, snaked a huge vein upon which protruded a large, flesh-colored mole that glowed crimson as the vein writhed with her fury.

Sister Geralda wore wire-rimmed spectacles imbedded into her eye sockets as if she had toppled into them face first from a bit of a height. Were her teeth really yellow and snaggled? Did she have bad breath? Did her upper lip lift and crimp on one side when she smiled? Yes. These things are true; but I do not share this with my audience. Memory: so seductive, like a drug. With my chemistry and history, I have to be decidedly circumspect with it.

With the note in my hand, I walked up the stairs, past the mammoth statue of the Virgin Mary, to the second floor and knocked on Sister Geralda's door. No answer. I knocked again. No answer. I stood out in the hall for what seemed a long time, wondering what to do, getting a little panicky. I knocked again. This time the door vaulted open and there stood Sister Geralda, dipped in black capes and smiling down upon me. Behind her, the bulbous eighth graders, like Swift's Brob-dingnagians, stuffed their little desks. I must have appeared to them most outlandish. They looked befuddled, as if unsure whether to run or stew me in a pot with vegetables.

"Were you going to stand out in the hall all day, Mr. Bathanti?" Sister Geralda demanded.

The nuns, especially Sister Geralda, had perfected a line of Socratic inquiry to which any response would render one an idiot. Whether a roughed-up or simply disgraced idiot was entirely arbitrary.

"No, Sister," I answered.

"'No, Sister?'"

"Yes, Sister."

"'No, Sister?' 'Yes Sister?' Which is it, boy?"

The eighth graders broke rank and howled. Sister Geralda wheeled on them. They hushed on a dime, hands immediately refolded over their inkwells, eyes straight ahead on the mute Christ crucified above Sister Geralda's steel desk.

Turning back to me, she said almost sweetly, "Knock on the door and enter. That is how you do it, Mr. Bathanti."

"Yes, Sister."

"Now you may try it again."

"Yes, Sister."

Relieved, I walked back into the hall and closed the door behind me. Then I rapped twice and entered the room.

"Yes, Mr. Bathanti?" said Sister Geralda.

"I have a note for you from Sister Sarah, Sister."

She took from me the folded note and read it. She dragged me to her desk, bent me over it, and began flailing me with a board she had whipped out of nowhere. I had, in essence, delivered my own death warrant.

My audience, though shocked, I'm sure, laughs. A kind of nervous laughter, but laughter nonetheless. And, truly, it's okay. Smiling—my habitual response to a beating—I've given them permission to laugh: Charlie Chaplin squashed by the falling safe.

"It was the instant I first understood irony," I quip, and this brings the house down.

Shuffletown

In Shuffletown, Joan and I lived in a tiny yellow cottage with floor to ceiling windows along its southern face. It looked out on Highway 16: two dozing lanes of blacktop, north out of Charlotte, 741 feet above sea level, about a quarter mile from the Catawba River Bridge and the Gaston County line. At dawn, sunlight swept through the naked panes and spilled through the house. We'd watch it pool in the front room, have tea, then go back to bed.

When we woke, we hiked down to the river and floated on cheap blow-up rafts. On the water loomed Laura's Rozzelle House, a mammoth, antebellum, three storey shotgun house where you sat at a table with strangers and ate off the same platters: fried chicken, country ham, red-eye gravy, crabapple jelly, cathead biscuits.

The famous Shuffletown Dragway was a quarter mile south. Every night, we heard its revving engines and the whistle of burning rubber; and, in the lone autumn and winter we hid out in Shuffletown, glimpsed through the stripped trees the burning headlights of the jacked-up suicidal Falcons and Chevy IIs.

We were happy living in Shuffletown, renting by the month for $165. No one knew who or where we were.

Directly across from our yellow house listed a forgotten nameless country store with a couple of dead Pure pumps in the rutted gravel lot. The spindly rusted carcass of a Depression Ford tractor, like a preying mantis, leaned against the side of it.

On the other side: a rotted, sooty bay, years of grease on its black kaleidoscopic floor, out of which launched towering sunflowers.

The owner had wiry hair, the color of rye whiskey, bristling out of a Detroit Tigers baseball cap. Broken nose. Hard-lived and handsome before God and women. The blue eyes of a good man who had failed at doing good things. Decent teeth. A scar under his left eye. Two heavy days of red clay beard he aimed to shave. A flannel shirt and jeans. Beat cowboy boots. A cigarette in his mouth, or smoldering on the counter, often forgotten, scorching another brown caterpillar into the rough wood patina. Cigarette smoke cloaked him, and the smell of sweetish raw tobacco.

I imagined him wholesale, even then: the conflated archetype of every slick country boy rounder I'd run up on out in the Southern wild and had the pleasure of knowing. I tend to like that pedigree—a hapless good guy, a dreamer, just trying to make a buck, firing up one Lucky after another. In my neighborhood, back in Pittsburgh, his doppelgänger huckstered out of an automobile trunk suits and shirts, cigarettes and nylons, and made petty book in his cellar on weekends. An Aces guy, all the way, born athlete and poet: visited his mom every Sunday. But I knew this Shuffletown fellow best from a prison yard where he had likely paced in green fatigues waiting to max out after his latest bone-head jolt: cars or women, his fists—all three. Booze for certain.

This fellow sold cigarettes, hoop cheese and slab bacon, pork rinds and crackers, sodas and beer, big yellow net sacks of roasted Georgia peanuts. STP, Penzoil, maple syrup, chow-chow. This and that, whatever he latched onto in one of his quests: tack, even a couple of saddles, live bait, a pinball machine. One of the tired books in the short shelf he had for sale was *A Farewell to Arms*. He carried fruitcakes and beautiful packs of Bicycle playing cards in blue and red paisley packages. All of it: as if he had salvaged of another senescent store its inventory moments before its evanescence and simply threw on his floor and counters its estate. A gauze of dust shrouded everything.

I liked him and I think he liked me. As if I were an outlaw too—I felt at the time I was and wanted more than anything to be anonymous—and he understood that like him I toted my own trove of secrets, that I'd never make trouble for him. I didn't have a warrant on me, but he might have. He had no name, though surely we introduced ourselves, but just as likely not. He was 50; I was 27 and pined to be, more than anything, a writer.

We'd exchange pleasantries: weather, *how you getting along, have a good one, yes, sir,* the parsed out code of anonymity, live and let live, let the dead bury the dead. Neither of us wanted trouble. We were united in this. I paid him for miraculous six packs of Carling Black Label he pulled near frozen from under the counter upon which perched, like a gryphon, an ancient sixty-five pound battered chrome Burroughs cash register. Of course, he didn't have the proper documents to sell me beer, but I reckon, along with what regard he may have had for me, he figured me as well for a rube, an unwashed Yankee boy who didn't know any better—I hadn't been in the South long and my inflection betrayed me—and I was glad to play along for beer and Wise potato chips, and candy bars just across the scored blacktop from our pretty little house that no one at all knew about.

Joan and I were his only customers. He called her *Little Lady* and was sweet on her. We never glimpsed another soul cross his threshold. Then one day the place was padlocked and empty and took on instantly the look of long-time abandonment—a specter store that upon occasion mysteriously quickens, back for a new run, its proprietor from another realm and time; then fades in quietude like mist on the glass, without ado or announcement, receding into the misty kudzu—marooned in the solemn country along what was once a pig-trot.

Not long after the store quit, Joan and I were awakened by a deafening explosion that shook our house. When I opened my eyes, the room was white with unearthly light, then went black like the switch on the world had been yanked. I was certain we had been bombed. Joan woke crying, scrabbling in the pitch for her gown, tangled in the bedclothes. I hustled her out of bed through stinking clouds of smoke, out the front door, into a tempest crackling with electricity. A massive pine tree lay across the hood of our '66 Fairlane. We stood in the deluge holding each other, the haunted store across 16 flickering spastically in the voltage like a holograph.

We went back in the house. I grabbed a flashlight. The house smelled charred and smoky, but there was no fire. The switch-plates and receptacles had been blasted from their moorings. The walls were scorched. The light fixtures had detonated, glass strewn across the floors. We'd been struck by lightning.

It was in the living room of the yellow house, December 8, 1980: I was watching *Monday Night Football* when Howard Cosell abandoned his brilliant play-by-play and broke to the world in a stricken theatrical voice the heart-stopping news that John Lennon had been shot four times in the back. It was the

Feast of the Immaculate Conception. The store had been closed for months by then. Eventually, we were evicted.

Your Mum and Dad

They fuck you up, your mum and dad.
They may not mean to, but they do.
They fill you with the faults they had
And add some extra just for you.
　　　　　—Philip Larkin, "This Be the Verse"

My parents hail from a generation which insists upon arriving at least an hour before every assignation, where being on time has a divine imprimatur. Thus we pull into the Charlotte airport well before their return flight to Pittsburgh. They have been with us for two weeks—their annual spring trek to visit, where they exchange the routine of their household for the routine of ours. The key difference, of course, the rarifying element, is that in our house live children; and my parents literally worship children, especially their grandchildren.

A big-game apprehension attends the visits of my parents. Preparation is everything. Practice is long and grueling. To take this analogy a little further, my wife, Joan, is head coach and tactician. With her at the helm, we manage a year's worth of sprucing and repair in the two weeks or so before my parents cross our threshold. My mother is legendary for the antiseptic cleanliness of her house, and it is apparently daunting, for a woman, at least, to have such a mother-in-law.

Joan storms the house like Vince Lombardi, and there is no choice for the boys and me but to do her bidding. I console myself with the fact that these are things that have to be done—should have been done long ago—in any event. Closets and cabinets are cleaned out and rearranged, new towels hung from the bathroom dowels, new sheets on the guest bed. Garages and outbuildings are swept and tidied, grass mowed, shrubs and spring flowers edged and mulched, and a dogwood tree planted. There are innumerable trips to the county landfill. This year I rent a pressure washer and clean the outside of the house, use the lethal water-jet to strip the old paint from the front porch; then, wearing a surgeon's mask and dragging an extension cord with a caged light bulb, put two coats of toxic, barn-red paint on it in the middle of the night; trowel on roofing cement around the chimneys' flashing; replace the steps on the back porch and coat them with a mold retardant; buy primer and aluminum paint and brushes for the outbuilding roofs, and Sakrete to point up the brickwork around the outside vents.

But time, mercifully, runs out. The final details before fetching my folks at the airport are rake out the fridge, clean the oven, scour the bathrooms and kitchen, put a vase of fresh flowers on the new-tablecloth-covered kitchen table, vacuum, and clean out the car which has already been to the carwash. The house looks great. The new lamp in the living room, the new carpet in the dining room, the new bookshelves and car-pets in the boys' rooms, the new throw rugs everywhere, the new hanging baskets on the front porch, the new stuff I don't even know is new, and the pastel box of Kleenex for my parents' bathroom. The very last thing, as I nose the car toward Charlotte, is Joan's admonishment that I not even remotely let on to my mother that she's gone to any preparatory fuss what-soever. Then she immediately passes out, having stayed up all night cleaning.

This visit came off against all odds. Six days before my parents were to arrive, the last of my mother's brothers, Uncle Dick, had a heart attack. Early reports were encouraging, but "it destroyed his body," as my mother said, and he died two days later. So, after spending two days at the hospital, three days at the funeral home, then the next morning attending the funeral and my sister's daughter's high school graduation that same night, my mother and father on the following day boarded a plane for North Carolina.

The second we have them buckled into the car, they fall asleep. When we finally get back home with them, an hour later, we see from a distance parked in our front yard a yellow bulldozer and a backhoe. Of all days, the county has today decided to bury new cable. Along the edge of our freshly clipped emerald lawn a ditch, flanked by yard-high bunkers of red clay, has been gouged. Our yard looks like a construction site.

Our ritual first order of business is to inventory the food my parents have hauled along with them from Pittsburgh: salami, pepperoni, olives, Fontinella, Jarlsberg, Provolone, Pecorino Romano, Tara Lucias and pizzelles my mother baked, and pizza shells and fresh loaves of Italian bread from Rimini's Bakery which my father points out were still warm when he fetched them at five o'clock that morning. We spread it all out on the kitchen table and sit down and eat too much even though dinner time is not far off. Whatever the kids want, we say yes to: another Tara Lucia, another chunk of cheese. Watching them eat gives my parents so much pleasure it borders on the pathological. "God love their little hearts," my father says at the bulging jaws of his grandsons.

As if his ecclesiastical respondent, my mother intones, "God love them both," and drops more cookies on their plates.

After eating, the kids know to trip into Grammy and Pap's room for their presents: books, balls, Legos® clothes. There is another round of kisses and embraces. We all know that, really, this is the best part of the visit, and hang onto its perfection as long as we can.

Then, heading to the kitchen to get the traditional first-night pizzas ready for the evening meal, Joan and I leave my parents to settle in. I hear their voices behind the door, just the sound of them, pleasant and tired, the way I used to as a child, and for a moment I feel that same ineffable well-being and safety. A little later I tiptoe back in to get my jeans out of the closet and find them asleep on top of the spread, lying on their sides like babies. Their opened suitcases, side by side, rest neatly in a corner, their prescription bottles regimented on the dresser, my father's razor on a folded white washcloth next to a can of Right Guard. On the wall above my mother's head is her framed high school graduation portrait taken in 1936. In it she is indisputably beautiful. I look down on her as she stirs, a handkerchief clutched in one of her hands.

At supper we chat a bit about Uncle Dick. My mother is sorrowfully resigned, but she really seems fine, just tired. I have to give it to her; she's tough. A funeral and a commencement in one day, then a plane ride the very next morning. Somehow we get to talking about Jimmy Longo, a neighborhood guy who used to pick up and deliver our dry cleaning back in Pittsburgh. We have a few laughs at his expense, and then I relate a story he told me the last time I had seen him. Jimmy was bowling and he set his Styrofoam cup of coffee down on a bench. A great big black guy—the fact that the guy was black being the *coup de grace* for Jimmy—accidentally sat on it. The story itself wasn't funny, but to see and hear Jimmy, a twitchy tiny guy with a big nose and big hat, relate it, deadpan and with a little bitterness over the lost cup of coffee, was hilarious. I do my best to imitate him: his voice, the way he repeats phrases like "I mean, Jesus Christ, he sat right on the goddam cup of coffee," a hand flying up every few seconds to punctuate his outrage.

But, as my mother laughs, something misfires. A shade in her circuitry. An eye closes. In the other, a silver asterisk fizzles before that lid flutters, falls, and her head lolls back. Her body flops limply in the chair. My mother is dying. I know this is true because I'm utterly detached and able to accept it. Like a curse. Not scared, not frantic, though by now we are all calling, hailing her back from wherever she's gone, my father on his feet, slapping her hand.

"Rose, Rose," he barks, more frightened than I've ever seen him.

I'm already picking through the bones of what this will mean to me for the rest of my life: how I killed my mother, made her laugh until she died. I, alone, who pushed her to this on such a night as this in front of my family. In front of my wife and children and my father. My nightmare premonition come true like some twisted fairy tale that was my childhood: the bad boy who killed his mother. *See, see,* she's already saying from the grave. *I warned you. You never know when to let up.*

I hope it is my voice which summons her, my tenderly inflected, urgent *Mother,* prompted only by extremity. As she opens her eyes, and looks at me as if I've stolen her from a spell, I'm at her side, holding her hand which I lift and kiss quite unconsciously. It appears I love her.

By now Joan has called 911, and my mother is already protesting that she is fine; she doesn't need "any 911."

The Rescue Squad arrives in a hoopla of lights and sirens. The dogs go crazy. I am waiting at the door. Two of them are ex-students of mine, a benefit and hazard of teaching at a small college in a small town. I introduce them to my mother who eyes them with bored imperiousness. She is fine, as she has said now more than once, and does not appreciate any of this. We finally think to pry the traumatized, bug-eyed children from their seats and shoo them off to play. Everything checks out, and my mother is pronounced "okay." Probably hyperventilated is all, say the EMTs, but a little trip to the hospital just to make sure wouldn't hurt.

My mother raises her hand as if to swear an oath—a gesture built into the family DNA—which means that discussion has terminated, and says, "No."

Joan and I walk the EMTs to the door and thank them. I shake hands with my students. One of them says, "You don't give A's, do you?"

The other says, "I hate writing."

When we return to the dining room, my mother is clearing the table and my father looks like he has just lost an argument.

After the children are bedded, we end the night with television. Since we very rarely watch TV, we do not subscribe to cable and its smorgasbord of useless channels. We have, alas, only network stations, and their reception is rather scattershot as a result of our choice to live out in the country, a decision on our parts regarded as dubious by my parents. They have been visiting now since 1976, and each year we go through the same discussion about what channels we do and do not get. The network channels in Pittsburgh are 2, 4, and 11, plus my parents of course have cable. What idiots wouldn't?

When we ask what they would like to watch, they volunteer what they routinely watch at home, but wistfully append that, here in Statesville, North Carolina, where they currently find themselves, Channels 2, or 4, and 11, the Pittsburgh channels, are unavailable. This is true, I say patiently, but we do get channels 3, 9, and 36 (although 9 is the only one that actually produces an identifiable picture). We just have different numbers.

"We don't have to watch anything," my mother says, clearly disappointed.

"Yeah, let's watch something," I say.

"If you were home, what would you be watching?" Joan asks.

"You don't have to watch it just because of us," says my mother. "Do they, Joe?" to my dad.

"Nah, nah, we don't care," he responds.

"Sure," urges Joan. "Let's look at something."

We finally settle on one of the news magazines. *20-20,* perhaps. One segment is about a kid raped by his little league coach, another about genital mutilation, and the last is a little treatise on masturbation. My parents, before they both almost instantaneously fall asleep, *tsk-tsk* all the while about what a horrible world their grandchildren are growing up in. Every few minutes, my mother snaps out of her doze. Finding my father asleep on the couch beside her, she indignantly nudges him awake before nodding off again herself. But should we switch off the television, it is as if the *Angelus* has boomed in their ears. Rapt attention: *What happened to the TV?* It is in this absurdist manner that Joan and I are held hostage night after night by the insidious TV while my parents sleep through their favorite shows.

The airport is packed. I've never seen it so crowded. My father and I muscle into the long baggage check line, while my wife and two little sons, along with my mother, trail far behind. My mother is all but crippled with arthritis, Spinal Stenosis to be precise. Even so, the constant pain she lives with, the inner domineering affliction the rest of us can only guess at, will not brook much in the way of others' solicitousness, nor allow her to admit to it. When they catch up with us, I am astonished to hear that my wife has somehow convinced her to ride a courtesy cart to the departure gate, nearly half a mile away.

Like a bodyguard, I hover close to my dad. Just the day before, my mother had remarked that he was getting old. She and I had driven home from her hair appointment. My father, smiling, in T-shirt and shorts, sat in a chair in front of our opened garage. At his feet played my boys. At that very moment, I had imagined him happy until my mother made her observation—very matter-of-factly with a note of wonder and tenderness in her voice which then, I swear, tailed off into a wistful internal monologue replete with all the images of their genesis as lovers. But they are clearly lovers no longer, and I suspect my mother's pronouncement is commentary enough on her own mortality, though she looks good, well younger than her seventy-seven years. She sees in looking younger great virtue, an accomplishment, intrinsic worth.

But my dad, pushing eighty-one, looks good too. He wears a flat cap, plaid shirt, khakis and a very cool pair of Nikes. He chews gum and rattles his change. I'll be glad to look like him when I'm eighty-one. In the past few years he has literally walked out of, *walked* out of, surgery for cataracts, a ruptured Achilles tendon and reconstructive knee surgery—albeit in the latter two cases on crutches. But my mother is right; he is getting old and I cleave to him at the airport because, just like my mother, there is literally less of him. I am larger than my father, taller, broader, stronger, faster. This is of course inevitable, a fact of life, but this inversion of the old father-son paradigm still imbedded in my psyche requires, at least on my part, some adjustments. As I watch my father hand his tickets to the young baggage clerk, I am watching myself.

The clerk, terribly official, pompadoured, sophisticate, well aware of the gravity of his position (I've inherited my mother's causticity), asks to see a photo-ID, which my father produces from the only wallet I've ever known him to own. He still carries in it his original Social Security card—from 1938. I see myself again in the photograph on his driver's license.

"Since you entered the airport, have you accepted anything from a stranger?" the clerk asks my father.

"No. I haven't."

The clerk stamps the tickets, returns them and the license to my father, who steps closer to the counter, smiles and adds: "I never accept anything from strangers."

This type of aside, when he is on the road, is irresistible to my dad. He likes people and this is his way of establishing communion. He is aware also of his senior citizenship which entitles him to a kind of ease with younger people. They have a lot to learn from him and he likes to be liked. Unlike my mother who sees insularity as strength, familiarity somehow as capitulation. She chides him for these jaunty stabs at worldliness. In response, the clerk attempts a smile, but has already started waiting on the next flyer.

My father turns to me: "They have to ask you that now." *Now* as though to underscore this harrowing world in which we live, as opposed to the one of 1938. I nod and worry not so much about the lethal times in which I must bring up my sons, but if they'll have things to talk with me about when I'm an old man. The fact is that my father and I are a little embarrassed—not by intimacy itself, but by having to talk in the first person about it to each other. Over the years we have remained, like Nick Carraway and his father, "unusually communicative in a reserved way."

When I was eight years old and playing Little League baseball, I had to fill in one game for our catcher who was hurt. The opportunity excited me until I was told by my dad, the team coach, that I'd have to wear *a cup*. "For protection," he said. That was the sum of the explanation. I was puzzled. How does one wear a cup? And to protect what? Wouldn't I be protected by the traditional "tools of ignorance?" What kind of cup? I pictured an entire array of cups: coffee, tea, Dixie, demitasse, deathcups. I couldn't quite equate any of these vessels with apparel, much less protection. I finally settled on a loving cup—don't ask me why—the kind I had seen on TV handed to jockeys when their horses won the Kentucky Derby.

There I was in my mind's eye behind the plate. In addition to mask, chest protector and shin guards, there was a golden trophy on its marble plinth standing guard before me. That this tableau is ludicrous goes without saying; and what it might signify that I conjured it I couldn't say; although thinking about it for the first time in thirty-seven years, I guess I had, even back then, without really knowing it, begun to fear castration. At any rate, this is what I had decided *cup*, in this context, meant. And no further information had issued from my father.

Nor did I ask questions. Even though burning with curiosity, I didn't want to hear whatever explanation my father might deliver. Finally presented with the actual *cup*, I was confused and horrified. More than anything, it looked to me like the contraptions through which fighter pilots in movies took in oxygen. Beige plastic, its rim padded in rubber, it was accompanied by a medicinal-smelling jockstrap with a marsupial snap pouch inside of which the thing was secured and snapped. The entire affair was then slipped on like a codpiece.

When faced with my look of utter incredulity, my father had muttered, "For your pee-pee." God, at that mortifying moment to have been shed of my "pee-pee," my "privates," my "weenie." Oh, just to have had a good old-fashioned penis, or even a fig leaf. But the commandments guarding purity are not injunctions against "pee-pees," which are after all cute, harmless, and frequently powdered. A penis, on the other hand (so to speak), is a hirsute sexual tool and herein lies the dilemma. Did the fact that key information regarding my cup was withheld have anything to do with where it resided on the body? Had it offered knee or elbow protection, would my dad have been so reticent to explain?

After that first experience behind the plate—the cup was terribly uncomfortable, painful and embarrassing—I never wore it again. I stashed it in a drawer, and was never asked about it. Like lots of things stashed in drawers, it eventually disappeared. I have a vision of my mother spiriting it off to the backyard trash with ice tongs.

There is, however, something very comforting in my father's silence. As a high schooler, my first few forays into cheap wine left me so besottedly drunk and incoherent that I only made it home because my guardian angel was a teetotaler. Inevitably, I ended up swooningly ill, vomiting uproariously into the cold cellar's toilet, as far away from my parents' bedroom as I could get. When my dad suddenly appeared to see what in the world was going on—never my mother, thank God—I'd confess that maybe I'd eaten one cheese steak too many; maybe it was that fifth milkshake. Whatever. He never interrogated me, the stench of regurgitated wine notwithstanding. He never said anything, just reached over and flushed the purple water off to Orpheus, asked me if I wanted some Brioski to settle my stomach, then walked me back to my bedroom as I stumbled up the two steep flights in what I was sure was stone-cold sober fashion.

One time my father popped into the house unexpectedly while I was trysting with a girl. I had time only to spirit her and her effects into my closet, hop back into bed and feign an illness-induced nap. He marched right into my room—the door had been open—and peered down at me. Feeling like the narrator in Poe's "The Tell-Tale Heart," I mumbled pitifully, "I don't feel very good." When I opened my eyes, I saw behind him on my desk a pile of earrings, bracelets, necklaces, hair barrettes, and a vial of perfume that clearly did not belong to me. My father turned and looked at them—I swear he did because I saw him in the mirror above the desk—then, without inquiring why I wasn't well, without saying the first word, he walked out, shutting the door behind him.

Another time, after I had been married for a year, my father had to come into my old bedroom where Joan and I were just waking. He knocked and we told him to come in. My mother had sent him up to fetch Scotch tape from one of my desk drawers. No problem. Except that Joan and I suddenly remembered in utter panic that in the drawer he opened, right next to the tape, was a little baggy of marijuana. He grabbed the tape, bid us good morning, and took off. There was no way he couldn't have seen the contraband.

Maybe my dad didn't come through on the cup, but more importantly to me, even now, he didn't devastate me when he had not only numerous opportunities, but every right to. He held off doing a job on me because he thought holding off, in those cases, would be better. For me, they were. I no longer vomit in the basement, or secrete women in my bedroom, and hide marijuana in my parents' home. I don't know what might have happened if he had confronted me. Maybe he was just trying to spare me, and himself, embarrassment, as in the case of the cup.

There is only one time I have seen my father embarrassed, and it was also on that occasion that he apologized to me for the one and only time since I've known him. I was eleven or twelve. He and I were cruising down Highland Avenue in our two-toned rose Rambler. My dad has always been a cautious driver, so he was able to brake and barely swerve to avoid the car that hurtled through the red light at Penn Avenue, and would have plowed into us on my side. This was pre-seatbelt America (cars came equipped with them, but no one ever thought of using them), so in emergency stops, my dad would rather zealously throw his right arm across his shotgun-passenger to keep him from smacking the dashboard. As he did this, pretty much knocking the wind out of me, he shouted at the driver, "Where in the fuck are you going?"

As if my breath hadn't already been literally snatched from me by the shock of seeing that speeding car bearing down on me, let alone the big forearm slamming into my chest. But the sound of that taboo word—the meaning of which I knew well, and had recently developed the habit of uttering among my pals—issuing from my dad's mouth, all but made me lose consciousness. I wanted to disappear. Whatever was to come next, I did not wish to be present for.

"Excuse my language," was all my father said, but it pained me terribly to hear him say it because I knew he was ashamed. I wanted to assure him that it had all been my fault—to protect him because he suddenly seemed so fragile.

While, over the years, we've extended advice to each other, we've spared each other lectures. Some things, it seems, we haven't had to talk about, as if the transcendent bond between us is silence. Faith that everything will be okay if we just shut up. Maybe, as a parent, as a child, you sometimes have to play dumb.

The rest of the family—my wife, our sons and my mother—wait for us in the golf cart. I walk with my arm around my dad. We get in and spin wildly off, our driver laying on the horn that sounds like police sirens in foreign films. Along the gleaming tiles, people stream all around us, up and down escalators, in and out of myriad restrooms, restaurants, bookstores and boutiques. They run. They laugh and cry. They push on, relentless, grim, euphoric. These wanderers of every incarnation, whose parents never told them the real story about how babies are made, in this huge Freudian house for a few relative instants. As we whip along, my mother announces the names of each establishment. "They have those in Pittsburgh," she declares.

There is not a lot of time before they board, and I am thankful of this. These leave-takings unnerve me. My mother, though not in the least the weepy sort, invariably cries, filling me with regret. Trying to dilate this last moment, I hold her in my arms and tell her that it won't be long until we are all together again. I'd tell her anything to make her happy since I know this life of silence—her way of loving—is breaking her heart for all she can't say.

And I, I am working up to telling them that I love them. Actually saying, articulating, formalizing in a sentence with a subject, verb and direct object, launching it through language out into the ozone where it will forever orbit and echo. *I love you* simply has not been something we've volunteered to one another in our nuclear family, and I don't believe it was said much, in that fashion, if at all, in my extended family. Birthday, Christmas, First Holy Communion cards and letters are signed *Love*. Chiseled into tombstones is the word *love*. Occasionally in a mood of maudlin bravado, one might literally utter, So-and-so sends *love*. But one would never look another in the eye and say "I love you." Not to your mother, father, sister or brother. Not to your wife or husband. I have never heard my father or mother say it to each other, nor my hordes of aunts and uncles, nor my friends' parents either. Never.

My parents, the children of immigrant parents, are still in shock from the Depression, World War II, and its aftermath. Their unrelieved half-century yokes—my father, a steelworker; my mother, a seamstress—would lead me and a good few of my rather pampered contemporaries to the existential ash-pile, if not to the cemetery, in a week. Fun and relaxation were absent from their lexicon. All they did was toil and scrape and sacrifice, so they could do for my sister and me. Each day of our lives, growing up, there were dozens of examples of their love, manifest in every breath and movement they made.

However, they never *said* to us, "I love you." But, of course, they didn't have books and talk shows and therapists urging them to articulate what I'm sure they felt was abundantly clear—as opposed to my generation which, almost defensively, throws "I love you" around like confetti.

My wife and I habitually, ad nauseum, tell our children that we love them. Certainly we want them to know this, but maybe more than this we are worried that they'll develop our neuroses, our insecurities, that they'll end up on the shrink's loveseat if we don't insist at least a hundred times a day that we adore them. As much as anything, finally telling my parents I love them is, for me, self-absolution; I've got to get this off my chest, get it over with. Besides, I do love them, and what if they die—they're getting pretty old—and I haven't told them?

I say it: "I love you, Mother. I love you, Dad."

They look at me like I need to get a grip, then assure me they love me too, love all of us. Why would anyone need to *say* it? Is there any question?

My wife is hugging them. The kids are shouting goodbye, holding on to them, petting them, kissing their legs, their arms, wherever they can park their lips. We huddle all the way to the hatch. My mother is crying. My father is laughing. "Goodbye," we croon. About us, a blessed communion of travelers and their entourages make of themselves similar spectacles.

Our custom is to remain in the terminal until their plane is airborne. This is a policy my wife has instituted and enforced. My reflex, once my parents step from my sight across that symbolic threshold, is to split, go home, begin to remand their visit to my own mythologized version. I also have a pathological aversion to waiting, even short waits.

"Let's leave," I blurt.

"Let's wait," Joan says.

"Okay," I say, thinking, of course we should wait, but still impatient to get out of there, actually beginning to feel a kind of closed-in otherworldly dread about being there. We press against the terminal windows, amuse the kids by pointing out the various routines of the ground crew, the planes coasting in, etc. Finally my parents' plane backs away from the terminal, heads for the turnaround and disappears.

As we await its takeoff, a serrated blade of lightning clips at the vanishing point of the runway. Far away—way out there. Where we are is okay. Not sunny, but decidedly not stormy. My parents' plane taxis leisurely into view, and lines up behind the half-dozen others also awaiting takeoff. Lightning again bisects the horizon. Then the muffled rumble of thunder; the wall of windows we look through shimmies.

We've already been here a while. I want to escape so badly I'm able to deny what is occurring. If my parents' plane can just get up in the air and beat this storm. But it is obvious that their necessary trajectory will take them right into the white band-saw that reveals itself in the blackening about it every thirty seconds or so. Quite clearly they will not be taking off terribly soon; and, again, there are several planes stacked in front of them, and now quite a few behind.

I ask the lady at the U.S. Air terminal what's going on.

"They're just waiting for the weather to clear," she says, smiling.

I sit back down and look out. Black as a prayer book. My parents already seem so gone. It's unbearably strange to know they are just beyond this glass at the edge of the firmament. It looks like hell out there. I turn away. A man with dyed, black, spiked hair and black, leather pants and a girl with a pierced septum sit in the same chair and make out ferociously. An old guy eating a hotdog ambles by and says loudly, "This is the worst hotdog I've ever eaten." A pilot, carrying his black box, walks by and, I swear, winks at my wife. "Just marry me," the boy in leather pants gurgles as he kisses the girl. I sneak another peak at the runway—sliced in half by lightning.

I get up and again ask the U.S. Air lady if she has any information. It's been a half hour since the flight was due to leave. She gives me the same spiel about the weather, but she seems pensive. Something must be up.

"They've turned the air conditioning off in the plane," she says.

I don't know why she tells me this and I don't know what it could possibly mean, but I start to worry. I find myself inside the plane with my parents, the stale air closing in, the sweating cabin growing smaller, mothers wrestling with crying babies. My mother is worked up.

"What's the matter?" she is saying to my father. "Something must be the matter. I can't breathe."

I want this sky to clear; I want this plane to take off. I want it to take off even if the sky doesn't clear. What I'm really afraid of is that the flight will be scratched and the passengers returned to the terminal. There will another infinite round of goodbyes. Perhaps my parents will have to come back home with us and repeat the visit. Repeat it again and again, like the transmigration of souls, until we get it right. *I love you* all over again. I don't have another goodbye in me. I want to go home.

Another twenty minutes go by. The kids have started going a little nuts. Running and turning somersaults. Mad giggling. An ambulance careens onto the tarmac with its hazards flaring. It has been summoned for my mother, I'm sure. Sitting in that stifling cabin with the lightening threatening to knife her, she's had a heart attack or stroke. I want to rush back to the U.S. Air lady and ask what the heck an ambulance is doing out there, but I'm too embarrassed to show my face again. It's my fault if she's dead, just like the Jimmy Longo story. Subconsciously I'm trying to kill her. Both of them. I want them to take off regardless of the suicidal weather because I don't love them enough to say goodbye again. It will be my fault if their plane crashes.

The ambulance, now with its hazards off, must be for someone else's parent because suddenly the flight schedule on the monitor lists my parents' flight as departed. The lightning has disappeared. In the ether, my mother and father are elliptical, rooted once again in what we've fabricated of one another.

"Let's go," I say.

Back home, delicate tendrils of neon green baby grass push through the straw covering the scarred front yard. Inside, the house smells mysterious, like it did the day I first walked into it. Built in 1915, the year my father was born, it is itself, outside of us. Like an empty church, solemn, silent, immaculate. Wandering into our bedroom, where my parents have resided for the past two weeks, I realize that this inscrutable hush enveloping the house is their absence, and now I miss them desperately.

Your Mum and Dad

My father has left for me on the dresser his Right Guard, with a fifty dollar bill under it; my mother, a bottle of Tylenol and the book she had been reading. I wonder if I will ever see them again.

Maz's Homer

Pittsburgh. 1960. October 13. A Thursday. In the final inning of what will be, by anyone's measure, a mythic World Series, the hometown Pittsburgh Pirates battle a venerable, unbeatable New York Yankees team that will go on to play in the next four World Series: Mickey Mantle, Roger Maris, Yogi Berra, Elston Howard, Whitey Ford, Casey Stengel.

Two months past my seventh birthday, I am in the second grade at Saints Peter and Paul School on Larimer Avenue, a street that cradles my family's identity in the new world. Sister Ann Francis, my teacher, whom I do not like at all, though she will not prove the worst of them, slips us word that Sister Geralda, the ferocious school principal, who also teaches eighth grade, has granted amnesty for the last ten minutes of the school day. We are to hurry home to witness the climax of the World Series.

Does Sister Geralda like baseball? I tend to doubt it, but I know nothing about her, nothing of what beats in her heart, nothing of what distinguishes her from the cruel and catatonic night face of the steely Allegheny River when our old Plymouth rolls across it over Highland Park Bridge. Nothing except that she paralyzes me with terror and, when I manage to cross her, she flails me unmercifully with a board.

Released, I run as fast as I can the entire way to my home on 430 Lincoln Avenue. My sister, a sixth grader, a kind and perfect girl, runs behind me. We blow in the kitchen door, whip by my mother into the living room, turn on the enormous Magnavox and fall into the couch.

Bill Mazeroski, a humble Polish-Catholic second baseman with the hands of a magician, leads off the bottom of the ninth for the Pirates. The score is 9-9. The seventh and final game of the deadlocked Series. The time is 3:36:30. Ralph Terry, the Yankees' fifth pitcher of the day, is on the mound. Maz takes Terry's first pitch for a ball, then cracks his next over the huge scoreboard in left field—still the only World Series-winning walk-off homer in baseball history—to win the World Championship for Pittsburgh. Church bells toll all across the city.

Never in my life have I witnessed such unadulterated celebration, such unanimous joy. The citizens of Pittsburgh stay up all night, beating on pots and pans, singing and dancing. The tunnels leading in and out of the city are impassable for the mountains of newspaper and confetti. It is a moment by which I will measure the rest of my life.

That home run remains one of the mileposts of my consciousness, a Station of the Cross. Clearly a miracle. As numinous as the Burning Bush; or The Feast of the Epiphany (from the Greek: *the appearance; miraculous phenomenon*) which commemorates the "revelation of God to mankind in human form, in the person of Jesus"—when the wise men, Caspar, Melchior and Balthasar, showed up in Bethlehem. It is a Holy Day of Obligation.

Epiphany has also a decided literary valence. James Joyce, of course, "extended the meaning of the word": a "sudden, dramatic and startling [moment] which [seems] to have heightened significance and to be surrounded with a kind of magical aura."

On the day of that epiphanic home run in 1960, my father, a millwright on the Open Hearth at Edgar Thomson Steel Works in Braddock, the first steel mill that Andrew Carnegie erected in the United States, was six days away from his forty-fifth birthday. He would live to double that age and then some and, for all those years to follow, very nearly half a century, he would claim that he and I (my sister is curiously absent from his account) were at Forbes Field the day Maz launched his epic homer.

Not only that. My father also recounted, year after year, without wavering from the facts as he saw them, the following narrative. As the Pirates came to bat in their end of the ninth, I stood and made a proclamation in a voice ethereal enough to somehow compel the attention of all 36,663 fans that day swelling Forbes Field. I imagine myself enveloped in a heavenly shimmer, a sudden eerie hush befalling the minions, as they turned as one to where my dad and I sat in General Admission. I, a seven year old prophet, gave warning that Maz would hit it out on the second pitch. And then, by God, he did.

Well, I truly like my father's version better than mine. It's a great story, much better than what really happened. In it, I share the stage with what is arguably the most famous home run in the annals of baseball. Indeed, my father elevates me to the story's protagonist, a little seer, nearly Messianic, who can predict miracles. And, I suppose, more than anything, I am flattered. It was a way for my father, a man who revealed through words little of what he felt, to reveal his love for me. In his recounting of that greatest day of all days in Pittsburgh Pirates history, the big story was not the 1960 World Series, or Bill Mazeroski, or the city of Pittsburgh. It was me, his only son, a measly seven year old, who emerged from it all a kid-prophet. "The version we dare to write is the only truth, the only relationship we can have with the past," writes Patricia Hampl. Which is true—unless we accept others' versions of the past. Like my father's.

But my father's version, if one may dispute a memory, is a figment. I was sitting on the couch next to my sister at our home on Lincoln Avenue. Yes, I watched that ball sail over Yogi Berra's head and into Schenley Park. But I watched it on television. Furthermore, my father would have never taken a day off work to go to a ball game. To do so, he would have lost eight hours pay, and forked out who knows how much for World Series tickets. He simply was not constituted thusly, period; and under no circumstances would my parents have allowed me to skip school for a ball game. I saw more baseball at Forbes Field with my dad than any other father-son duo I can drum up, but we were absolutely not at that one.

I don't know how many times my father recounted that story over the years—dozens—but I never once contradicted him—as much out of love and respect as anything. My father was pretty much the nicest man I've ever met and I can say in absolute truth (a word which this piece seems bent on discrediting) that he never once in the time we spent together on earth gave me a hard time unless I forced him into it. Not one gratuitous harangue or criticism. No meddling. I cannot remember once instance of his hurting my feelings. So it just was not in me to spoil what he fervently believed and gave him such pleasure to relive.

Another thing: he never told stories. The Mazeroski-home-run-prediction-tale is the only story I ever heard him spin, and I felt honored to be in it. Because I never piped up to correct my father—nor did my sister, leg to leg with me that day on the couch, nor my mother, at the kitchen sink when Maz connected—my father's memory of that day became family canon. The more I heard him tell it—with an uncharacteristic passionate verve, attention to detail, narratively nuanced in every way, and never differing, year in and year out—the more I began to weigh the two versions, mine and his, in terms of verisimilitude—even though, again, his version was false.

Yet my dad is a supremely more credible source than I. Anyone who knew him would attest to this. I rely on lying. In 1960, he had been forty-five and I a mere seven. Certainly his age bestows an authority to his recollection that a second grader cannot claim.

Could I have possibly been at that game and somehow repressed that memory? Am I secretly clairvoyant? "... not only have I always had trouble distinguishing between what happened and what merely might have happened," testifies Joan Didion, "but I remain unconvinced that the distinction, for my purposes, matters." Thus, it seems almost safe to say that I was there that day at Forbes Field, that I did rise and—in that gusty disembodied voice in *Field of Dreams* (a movie that, by the way, I do not like) that announces "If you build it, he will come"—predict that Maz was going downtown on the second pitch out of Ralph Terry's right hand.

In fact, I was there. The little Catholic boy, sacristan, acolyte, choir boy, in blue blazer with an emblem on his breast pocket of the Mater Dolorosa, white shirt and tie, next to a steelworker in a lime green asbestos jumpsuit and blue hardhat. That was me: the truant seven year old prognosticator people are still wondering what happened to.

This Bastard Day

March 4, 2001. The northeastern United States is buttoning up for a gigantic snowstorm. Despite these dire weather predictions, in which I have little faith, with my wife and two young sons, I have journeyed to Pittsburgh from my home in North Carolina to visit Philip DeLucia, my oldest friend in the world (since kindergarten), who is very ill.

From his seventh storey hospital window, I watch the snow belt down. One moment it isn't there, then at next glance it is. Miraculous and brutal. Stacked beneath it are neighborhoods I roamed as a boy, and a very young man: East Liber-ty, Shadyside, Garfield, Bloomfield, Highland Park. Where I went to school, played ball, had my first job, learned to drive on a 1963 blue Belair, kissed my first girl, learned about God's displeasure and mercy, committed sin after sin after sin, and was summarily forgiven.

When it is time for me to leave Phil, I embrace and kiss him. I tell him I love him, that he must rest and get better. I confide with passion a number of other things that occur to me, but they are only words. I walk from his bed and watch my wife, Joan, in a bright red blouse, lower herself over him like a blanket. They whisper. His hand is at the back of her head, stroking her brown, silver-streaked hair. Philip loves Joan very much, and she loves him. He and I both believe that she can bestow health. Surely, I think, this is how he'll regain his strength—from her touch, from the goodness and purity that haloes her. She can heal him.

One more time, I go to his bed to hold him and tell him I love him. Then we walk out of the room. Joan weeps. I look through Philip's cracked door. His head is turned to the black window. His eyes are closed. He looks like a child.

Outside the snow has turned to cold, piercing rain. Joan and I trot down to *Groceria Italiana*, two blocks from the hospital, to buy homemade ravioli, in Bloomfield, the last true Little Italy in Pittsburgh. So fiercely Italian, the parking meter poles are striped with the colors of the Italian flag. The old Italian women in the *groceria* make ravioli at a counter powdered with flour. They squeeze seasoned ricotta out of a pastry tube onto a wide expanse of dough, then cut circles of dough around the dollops and seal them with their fingers. The varieties are infinite, every kind of pasta imaginable. The kid working the register accepts my North Carolina check. A kindness that lifts me. I am that brittle.

It is Sunday. The Church of the Immaculate Conception is half a block from the storefront, but when we try its doors, it is locked. The rain beats down. I wear my father's hooded coat, but my wife is bareheaded and I want not one blade of this freezing rain to touch her, though she takes my arm and assures me that she doesn't care, it doesn't matter. At that moment, I resolve that I will buy her a red beret. More than anything, I am furious that Philip is lying in a hospital bed. But how do you kill the rain?

I am not one to call any day bastard, but this one… A cold and unforgiving bastard. A day it could take years to warm up from. As we cross the Liberty Bridge over the Monongahela River, I gaze through the windshield at the monochromatic city, dank and smoky gray, the fog-shrouded skyscrapers, steel sky pressing down on steel water, the banks ravaged by winter.

Rusted mill ruins, crawling with asbestos ghosts. Black rock wharves. Today, it is not my beautiful, beloved hometown, the Renaissance City, but what outsiders imagine of it, what it hasn't been for forty years. A city of eternal dusk, tiered in slag, belching fumes and ore dust. A lightless place the sun never penetrates.

A few flakes float down with the rain. Instead of going through the Liberty Tunnels, leaving the city and the river behind, we turn at the end of the bridge, just before the mouth of the tunnels, and drive up McCardle Roadway to Mount Washington, a precipice that looms over downtown Pittsburgh. In the nearly twenty-five years Joan and I have been together, we've never come here to stand as lovers and take in the fabled view which includes the union of the Monongahela and Allegheny rivers which birth the juggernaut Ohio.

At the observation deck, a few hundred feet above the skyline, we clutch each other as if the rail might give, and peer out into the iron mizzle. Once again, my life, each rite and sacrament, spreads in gloomy panorama: the entire city on the slow, swollen rivers, the epic gouge that was once Three Rivers Stadium, imploded and carted away as rubble. The city, heartsick, looks back at us, a man and woman hovering over it. As the temperature drops, and the ice knifes down on the souls locked inside this steel-town Sabbath, I can't help but feel compassion, love, for this impossible town and its faith to bear such weather, and still flower again each spring. At our backs hulks Saint Mary's of the Mount, but its church doors are locked too. The only candles we light this day for Philip are in our hearts.

At my sister's house, a Carolina blue University of North Carolina flag drapes the porch, in honor of my niece Katy, two months from graduation there. Inside, the last minutes of the Duke-North Carolina basketball game play on TV. On the stove is a huge pot of roiling water for the ravioli which we hand over to my mother.

It is good to be inside, out of the weather, safe and warm among family. I stand around, gape, pace and answer questions about Phil—he grew up in the house facing ours across one-way Collins Avenue—every now and then glancing out the window, until called to supper: wedding soup, salad, fresh Italian bread, roasted red peppers from my father's garden, ravioli, meatballs and sausage, grated parmesan. No *vino*—I would drink a bottle myself—because we have all offered it up for Lent.

Had anyone asked, I would have said I had no appetite, but to refuse food in an Italian family is high treason, or sign of profound melancholy reparable only by eating. There is simply no choice, so I eat and eat, as does everyone else around the table, and am grateful for every delicious, restorative bite.

Someone announces that it is snowing: "Really coming down." My mother, seated next to me on the left, lets out an involuntary gasp. Almost eighty-two years she's been fighting Pittsburgh winters, and still the occasion of snow unnerves her.

"*Jesu Christe*," she says, shooting a look at my father who eats happily at the head of the table. He is not worried about the snow, pounding down in earnest, the streets and yards and cars covered already by at least three inches.

My brother-in-law paces in from his vigil in front of the weather station. "New York could get two feet," he gravely announces.

There is still dessert and coffee with which nothing can interfere. It would be bad form to cut the meal short simply because of weather, but we eat with dispatch. My aged parents must be chauffeured home a mere mile and a half away, but over hilly, sometimes precipitous, unsalted slippery roads. This will fall to me. No other. Which is the way it should be.

In addition to alcohol, I am also denying myself sweets, so I excuse myself as the others finish. I take the stairs down to the basement, lift the garage door and walk outside. The snow rushes down, so fast that my sweater is coated in seconds. There are two more inches since last I looked out. Not a vehicle on the road. The burning streetlamps are hardly visible. The car is parked in the street. I start it, switch on the defrost and rear defogger, clear the wiper blades, begin brushing and scraping, then blindly pull the car into my sister's driveway. I find a snow shovel and scrape a path for my parents, a few crucial feet, from the garage to the car.

When I reenter the cellar from the garage, my parents are already making their way down the cellar steps from the kitchen. My mother has severe arthritis; under the best conditions, walking is a challenge. My eighty-five year old father comes in front of her, holding one of her hands and her purse. My sister comes behind. I stand at the bottom of the stairs ready to do what, if they fall, I'm not sure. My mother holds the handrail, says, perturbed, more than once, "I'm fine," and makes faces like: *If you'd all leave me alone, and get out of my way, I could make it safely down these stairs.*

Once we have her on the cellar floor, we shuffle slapstick like a rugby scrum toward the warming car.

"*Jesu Christe*," says my mother again when she steps out of the garage and the snow first hits her.

"Watch, Joe," she admonishes my father as he climbs into the back seat. "All you need is to fall."

"I'm watching, Rose," he replies.

"Don't get so cocky," she cracks.

I smile. My dad just shakes his head.

I exchange places with my thirteen year old son, Jacob, Philip's Godson, who has been standing with my mother. Carefully, so carefully, the way one handles a baby, I walk my mother over the shoveled path to the car and ease her into the front passenger side.

"Put on your seatbelt, Mother," I assert gently.

She sighs and grudgingly secures her seatbelt. The rest of the family stands out in the driveway, watching nervously like they might an experimental rocket launch. We must navigate three left turns, then a right, up and down hills, to get to my parents' apartment.

The first turn takes us up a vicious hill, and we quickly lose ballast. The car's back end spins out.

"Oh, my God," my mother mutters.

"We're okay," I say.

Beginning to wonder myself, I begin a didactic monologue to which my father, like a one-man Amen Corner, responds, "That's right," at key junctures. Pointers about driving in the snow, caution, watching the other guy, a host of clichés designed to calm everybody, chiefly me, as the car begins to lose ground and skid backwards down the glassy hill.

I shift from second into first. The tires catch for a moment, then wheeze, throw up a spray of slush, and we lose a little more ground. I throw it back into second, give it a little clutch so we don't stall—which would finish us—and we begin to inch back up the hill. Slowly, but steadily.

"Thank God," says my mother.

"Pump your breaks, Son," my dad chimes in.

"We're okay," I repeat, feeling the earth move in the proper direction beneath me, taking my hand from the wheel for just a split-second to pat the rosary in my pocket, aware that I've been deep in prayer.

There is a sacramental power in braving the snow, this pittance of danger, to drive my parents home. I realize, profoundly, in the caution I must observe to deliver them safely, that I love them. More now that they are old and depend on me. More now that I have a wife and children of my own who are waiting for me. That this inscrutable sacramental love is an outgrowth of the love I bear for my sick brother, Philip, whom I would happily carry over the snow in bare feet if it would cure him. But, for now, all I can do for him is deliver my parents home safely.

The snow itself is sacramental, an unexpected beauty and hazard, spilled stealthily from heaven when one least expects it. Like grace. Apparently, life really is precious. Perhaps that's why God dispatches danger. To allow us, beyond our own fears and existential dread, the blessed luxury of caring desperately for others. Even on a dank and dispiriting day such as this, we gathered around my sister's table to take into our bodies the nourishment that good cooking and the habit of family afford because we have faith in the healing, sacramental power of these offices.

When we reach the enormous apartment garage, my dad whips out the remote of which he is so proud, presses the button, and the huge aluminum door trundles up. Inside, I help my parents out of the car and we walk to the elevator that will lift them one storey to the carpeted hall that leads to their warm, well-lit apartment. They will not allow me to go a step further with them. They are fine. Now I must make my safe return. The city is filling with snow. To tarry is risk. They won't hear otherwise, and so I agree, touched as always by their worry. There is a round of *I love yous,* and exhortations for care and sweet dreams, then they rush me off, exacting from me a promise to phone the second I'm back at my sister's where my family and I are quartering.

Then I'm alone in the car, travelling slowly over the soft white earth, the snow flashing down like death, like life, and I am filled with gratitude. For my feet that regulate brake, clutch and throttle, for my hands that steer the car, for my mind that closes around memory, for the failure of my tongue to make language of it all, for the hovering pinions—the ones Philip in his grand passion grows—that beat above me, molting, minute by minute, this bastard day into Christ.

A Christmas Story

In early October of 1986, I was invited by the Anson County Arts Council to read a Christmas story, my choice, to the little children of the county on December 15 at the Hampton Allen public library in downtown Wadesboro, North Carolina. There would be hot chocolate, spiced cider, popcorn and snicker doodles. We'd sing carols, then decorate the library tree.

Of course, I accepted, flattered to be the centerpiece of such a well-intentioned, old-fashioned celebration, imagining fragrant children in red plaid jumpers, down leggings and rag-wool sweaters mesmerized at my feet as I delivered the season in earnest to them. My simple, but profound, gift to the county.

For the next two months, I went about my business as Anson Technical College's Writer-in-Residence: gigs with the Anson County Chapter of the D.A.R., the Norwood Book Club, the Worthwhile Book Club, Gum Springs Community Center. In the main, however, the bulk of my time was spent mounting a travelling holiday production of a most dubious one-act play called *The Christmas Dream*, by I.E. Clark, scripts of which were available, for a fee, from I.E. Clark, Inc. of Schulenburg, Texas. The play featured lines like, "My Master has come! My Lord is here. I know His voice!"

My newly pregnant wife, Joan; another pregnant woman, Julie; a recent transplant from Hawaii, Frank; and I were the cast, stage crew, truck drivers and engineers of various, somewhat cheesy, audiovisual pyrotechnics. Nevertheless, *The*

Christmas Dream charmed audiences at each county elementary school and nursing home we hauled it to, and my time remained wholly consumed by it. I hadn't really thought much at all about my Christmas appearance hosted by the Arts Council, much less engaged in any preparation until I saw my picture, along with the announcement of the looming program, the day before the event on the front page of the county newspaper, *The Anson Record*. I clipped the write-up and posted it to my parents in Pittsburgh. My involvement in such wholesome ventures swelled them with pride, though they always wondered, as they had with much of my professional life, why in the world someone would pay a grown man to do such things.

What I did prior to walking into the library on December 15 is a blur. I had originally remembered, rationalized, really, that I had been out of town the day of the reading, and had blown in at the last minute. However, my calendar for that year—I obsessively save them all, certain that someday they'll have archival importance—does not corroborate this. I had no other engagements on that date. Therefore I would have observed my routine day in the county. A run in the morning, then to the Hub, a popular country-cooking restaurant right on U.S. 74, the Andrew Jackson Highway, where in great peace and unadulterated joy I wrote and swilled righteous, working class coffee until lunch time. Then, deranged from caffeine, I picked up my wife at the Anson County Department of Social Services, where she served as County Day Care Coordinator and Problem Pregnancy Social Worker, and we cruised a mile down the four lane to Pizza Inn and ordered the salad bar.

In the afternoon, I'd have gone into my office at the College's storefront Community Services Division, right across from the library on Greene Street, and returned calls and correspondence and seen to whatever required my attention. One thing I do remember for absolutely sure was that when I left our house that morning of December 15, I was loaded with various Christmas treasuries and anthologies—supplied by Joan, who was educated and savvy in such matters—and was determined to read to my little charges that afternoon the very best Christmas story ever. But, for some reason, and here memory fails me entirely, I never got around to selecting the story until minutes before strolling, dressed in a coat and tie, into the library and seeing spread before me not only a brigade of glowing, expectant children, but many of their parents as well. And in the midst of them all sat my own sweet, lovely wife, sporting a black corduroy dress with a white bib, and looking for the first time, it seemed—though maybe it was holiday sentiment embellishing my senses—the least bit pregnant. She had left work an hour early to share in the merriment.

Despite my lack of preparation, I was ready. Clearly. I had always been a champ at pulling things off at the last minute. Not only that. I had in tow the perfect book: *Treasury of Christmas Stories*, edited by Ann McGovern. It was inscribed on the flyleaf to my wife by her mother: *Dear Joan, As I read this little book I could just "see" many wide-eyed girls and boys over many Christmases as you read its contents with the feeling and expression that come so easily to you.*

My mother-in-law's clairvoyant inscription inspired me with confidence. It even described perfectly my audience. Scrolling through the book, I came to a terrific illustration: a towering Christmas tree girdled in tinsel, ornaments swelling each bow. Gazing up at it in beatific wonder sprawled a model storybook family. The tale was "The Fir Tree," retold from Hans Christian Andersen. In the mere twenty seconds it took me to cross Greene Street from my office to the library, I congratulated myself that I had chosen the consummate tale without even reading it.

After being lavishly introduced, and a round of little hands clapping for the longest time, I pitched in, all ears myself, instantly relieved that the story started, "Once upon a time…"

"The Fir Tree," thank God, proved predictable enough— about a little fir tree leading an idyllic life out in the forest. His companions are the sun and fresh air, and other fir and pine trees. Occasionally little children from the village trek out to the forest and compliment him. But the little fir tree wants to grow into a big fir tree, which of course is not unusual in such stories, I noted, thinking with pleasure that this story would not only delight the children, but would in some way provide a moral for them as well.

The little tree grows tall, and as he grows he notices each winter that the largest trees around him are chopped down by woodcutters and carted away. This confuses him until the sparrows explain that the felled trees are taken off to houses and gloriously decorated for Christmas. The little tree, now no longer little at all, longs to be chosen for some family's Christmas. The winters pass and, finally, because he has become un-questionably the handsomest, tallest tree in the forest, he is harvested.

I looked up at my audience. Things were going great. The story had everything: memorable characters, exposition, rising action, conflict, and a decided sense of place. The kids— munching away, their gaping mouths crowned with hot chocolate mustaches, powdered sugar sprayed like snow across their cheery Yule outfits—had been sitting in suspense, wondering if our hero, the fir tree, was going to find a loving home. And when they could hardly bear it a moment longer, the little guy was delivered. The nippers were absolutely tickled. Their parents smiled fondly at me.

Rather than being elated at his adoption, however, the fir tree is sad. He reflects that he'll never see again the bushes and flowers and birds. Nevertheless, once festooned with Christmas gifts, candy, fruit, and lit candles, then stationed in the middle of the his adoptive family's parlor with a golden star at his tip, he reflects it is all "too splendid for any words to describe."

It occurred to me at that point that the tree is a tad manic, but the kids out there on the library floor, after a little droop at the tree's moment of existential despair, seemed completely happy again. And so are the kids in the story, so happy in fact that they get a little rowdy and one of the fir tree's branches is set afire by a tipped candle—which is quickly snuffed. No damage whatsoever. But then the children roughly pull presents from the tree's foliage and, in so doing, crack its branches. Once they have their hands on the gifts, they forget about the fir tree and he is plunged again into despair. Yet, he consoles himself that the next day he will surely be the center of another celebration.

Unfortunately, the next morning the servants drag the tree to an attic and leave him there in the dark. I chanced a look at my audience. The kids appeared a little puzzled. The parents too. A little setback, I figured, supremely confident in my mother-in-law and Hans Christian Andersen. The bipolar fir tree wouldn't be locked long at all in that spooky attic.

The tree, a bit of a basket-case at this point, remains alone and in the dark for what must be months. Trying to hang in there, he rationalizes that maybe the family stashed him in the attic to shield him from the harshness of winter, that come spring he will be replanted. He makes friends with the rats and mice by telling them stories about his days in the woods, but soon they tire of the stories and snub him. Reflecting on his misspent youth, the tree grows understandably maudlin, then out and out depressed—morbidly so. As did my audience.

There remained only a page and a half in the story. Even so, I held to hope. I mean, what kind of sick author would do this to a little fir tree? Not Hans Christian Andersen. He'd pull it out in the bottom of the ninth. When I looked up to smile, I noticed the children were deeply concerned, some catatonic. Their parents looked murderous. I knew I was in trouble when I glanced at Joan and she lip-synced, *What are you doing?* and then just shook her head.

Faith, I told myself, and forged ahead. What choice did I have? Well, the fir tree is finally released from the attic and into the sunny springtime yard "right next to a garden where fragrant roses hung over the fence and lindens were in bloom." He is filled with joy, and so was I, as well as my audience, for a split second, until we learned in the next sentence that his branches are "withered and yellow." Yet, he still wears the gold Christmas star which, suddenly, one of the bratty kids from the house rips away, just before stomping him literally to pieces.

I refused to lift my head from the text, but I heard whimpering as I read on. I felt especially, like a palpable force threatening to blast me off my stool, my wife's incredulity. She was hoping, I'm sure, that the child she carried would have none of my flair for judgment, if she was that charitable in her assessment of my idiocy.

The fir tree, at the bitter end, cries out, in the spirit of Franz Kafka's Gregor Samsa in "The Metamorphosis," "'But 'tis all over now.'" By then, some of the traumatized children were crying openly. Their parents, leveling homicidal glares at me, rushed to comfort them. As if it hadn't been bad enough, the tree, what's left of him, is chopped up and set on fire.

Blind Angels

The angel went dragging himself about
here and there like a stray dying man.
> —Gabriel Garcia Marquez, "A Very Old Man with
> Enormous Wings"

Pittsburgh, at the end of another terribly hot day in an unend-
ing string of terribly hot days, is a forge, the air like damp tepid
gauze, the people on the streets looking stretched, desperate,
short-tempered. My poetry reading, one of the events in the
eighteen-day Bloomfield Sacred Arts Festival—commandeered
by Philip DeLucia, my communion partner, my older son's
Godfather, my oldest pal on earth—is in the Bloomfield Art
Works, a small, un-air-conditioned gallery on Liberty Avenue.
On its walls is sacred art, comprised essentially of angels:
paintings, photographs, and drawings. They possess that
characteristic ethereal androgyny, and feathery beauty that has
become cliché. Still they are intriguing, though, in the main,
I'm tired of angels.

I'm stationed on the street in front the gallery. In a few
minutes I will enter it. In front of an audience that includes 26
members of my family from my father's side, most of whom
range in age from 73 to 93, I will recount, for the first time in
their presence, my version of the truth. If I were a smoker, I'd
have a cigarette. If I were a magician, I'd conjure a time when
cigarettes were charming and benign. Sixty years earlier, maybe,
when it would be expected of me, nearly 45 years old, and a

man of letters, albeit lower case, to lord here under this oppressive steel-town sky in a suit, white shirt, tie, a gray snap-brim fedora, and a gold watch upon which time unfolds in Roman numerals. Time which would be nothing to me.

If I were a magician, I would simply disappear. I would not walk back into the building and stand at the microphone, risking my entire identity among the people who have literally known me all my life. Bullshit, the rhetorician's ace-in-the-hole, will not fool any of these folks. They've changed my diapers. They've washed my mouth out with soap. They've kissed these mendacious lips.

I hesitate to say that I have always dreaded this moment. Dread is much too strong a word. This moment that in many ways I have striven for all my life. I have certainly anticipated it, but only in the abstract. When I take the mic, spread in front of me will be my entire extended family. Long-lived and fruitful, they swell the room. Not simply because there are so many of them, but also because they are a palpable force. Four generations of garrulous, gregarious southern Italians who have gathered here—exactly for what they don't know—my parents seated conspicuously in the front row. In addition there are my dearest oldest friends, most of them southern Italians themselves, guys I grew up with in East Liberty, and in some cases they've even hauled their parents in too.

Near impossible to get all these people together at one time, except for a wedding or funeral, this is the equivalent of a family reunion. Kissing, hugging, weeping, reminiscing. In and of itself, a performance, a great Fellini-like, Scorcesian burlesque which must run its course like a cattle stampede.

7:30, the starting time, comes and goes. Then 7:45, 8:00. Each time Phil thinks he has them herded up and almost seated, they break rank again to talk to someone they've only now spied. It is 8:15 by the time Phil brings the house to order. I have peaked, de-peaked and re-peaked. By now, standing out on Liberty Avenue, imagining myself elsewhere in a different time, I am merely peak-ed. I want to get this over with. After a long, dark night of the soul, the condemned's only solace is that his execution starts on time.

Up the street is Tessaro's Bar and Grill. A TV from its second-storey window catches my eye. The Pirates are playing. A man wearing the hometown black and gold swings at the pitch. The camera follows the flight of the ball until it reaches the wall where the opposing outfielder marshals for his saving leap. But the ball inches over his glittering glove. I hear my name coming at me from inside where Phil has just introduced me as his best friend. And everyone is clapping.

My reading is memorable only for the heat, the half dozen fans doing nothing but circulating hot swampy air. My family would rather be cooked than miss this dubious event; it is a matter of honor. In fact, my 89 year old Aunt Lucy purportedly had a mini-stroke mere seconds before leaving the house, but could not be dissuaded from attending. The mic, set up so the old people can hear, malfunctions. As I literally shout what strike me as my shamefully narcissistic poems, and watch the audience peer querulously at me as they fan themselves with their programs and strip off as much clothing as possible, little rivers of sweat run down my torso as my drenched white shirt grows heavier.

About me melt the angels, their smiles turning to grimaces. Like the rest of us, they have been remanded this evening to Purgatory. More than anything, they're bored. Mercifully I lose my voice and things shut down a few minutes early. With arms around my two oldest relatives, my father's sisters, Aunt Lucy and Aunt Gina, I walk out onto the avenue. During my reading they occasionally huddled in conference, then sang out chidingly whenever they judged a poem had strayed too far from the truth.

"You were always a good boy," Aunt Lucy says.

Aunt Gina retorts, "He was a bad boy."

I thank them and give them big kisses—just happy the whole thing is over and nobody died. After seeing off my wobbly beaming parents and aunts and uncles, cousins and great cousins—"My God, the heat," "I thought I was going to croak," "I was sweating gumdrops," "Did they ever hear of air-conditioning"—Joan, my wife, and I walk with my friends across the street to Del's, an Italian restaurant. Standing shakily in front of Saint Joseph's Church is a guy, dressed completely in sky-blue, clearly drunk, sipping from a quart of beer. He smiles and waves, and we all wave back.

One of the guys I'm with is Richard Infante, a buddy from high school and a writer himself, who helped Phil organize the Festival. Richard, relatively late in life, became a priest. I haven't seen or talked to him for years and years. He explains that he was late to the reading because he had been hearing confessions that afternoon. Suddenly talk swerves toward that most daunting of sacraments and someone remarks to Father Richard that in his role as Confessor he probably hears some pretty outlandish things.

"You wouldn't believe," he says.

We're all more than curious about the things he hears in the confessional.

"Little things like telling a white lie or having a nasty thought about your neighbor to really bad things," he volunteers. "Even crimes."

"What if somebody came in and told you that he killed someone? What about a murder or something horrible? What would you do?" Phil asks.

Without hesitation, Father Richard replies: "I am bound by my vows never to divulge what I hear in the confessional."

"What do you tell people who trot out these piddly little things like lying? Do you tell them to forget about it?" I ask, thinking of all the times as a child I had obsessed over tiny, inconsequential things I no longer consider sins. Human foibles. Congenital imperfections—inescapable, even endearing.

As a child, when I still looked upon the sacrament of Penance with utter gravity, sinning was inescapable. I became physically sick contemplating Confession. So sold on the fact that I was a bad boy, a pathological sinner, I was absolutely immobilized with terror at the thought of it. My Uncle Dick, on the eve of my first Confession, assured me that I'd be in the confessional so long, I'd better take my lunch; that, instead of the standard penance of a few Our Fathers and Hail Marys, I'd be sentenced with the Stations of the Cross.

Not only was a fledgling catechist required to list his sins, but to enumerate them as well. For instance: *I lied six times.* Or, my particular situation: *I lied 347 times.* I was snared. Had I only lied, or cheated, or disobeyed, whatever it might have been, a mere six times, I would have breezed through Confession. Of course, I never recalled how many times each offense had occurred—exponentially, in most cases. A literalist back then, as most children tend to be, I was not only distraught gauging precisely the quantity, the sheer freight, of my mortifying transgressions; but, more than anything, catatonic at the thought of admitting to my Confessor, an inch of my face, in a totally blackened box the size of a phone booth, that staggering sum. "Examining my conscience," as we were schooled to do by the nuns, resulted in a dizzying collision within my seven year old cranial vault between metaphysics and mathematics. *Sickness Unto Death. Fear and Trembling.* Only in second grade, I was a disciple of Kierkegaard without ever having heard of him.

On one occasion, I smuggled into the confessional a little booklet listing each potential sin, beside which I noted the number of how many times I had committed it. Inside the confessional, however, it was too dark to read, so I had to wing it. Taught by the oppressive, ever-chaste nuns, my chief tutors in matters of theology and spiritual fitness, I had been made into a hopeless neurotic over the sacrament of Confession. I was so preoccupied with the cleanliness of my soul that, at one point in third grade, I went to confession every day until Father Battung, the parish pastor, in a lacerating breach of confidentiality, called me by name and told me not to come back again for a month.

On another occasion Monsignor Hayes, when I confided it had been "a while" since my last confession, literally excommunicated me—loudly enough so that my classmates, waiting in line outside the confessional, heard clearly and were laughing when I emerged in disgrace, though chuckling myself.

By the time I turned 13 in 1966, the sacrament of Penance had simply become too much for me, a liability I could no longer abide, a masquerade I could no longer pull off. While I was innocent enough to get a Peanuts birthday card, commemorating my entry into teendom, from my sister, Marie, I was also in the throes of puberty. Suddenly I found myself possessed of sins I had to be shriven of if my spiritual health was to be salvaged. Not just venial sins, those misdemeanors seared off in Purgatory. But mortal sins, capital crimes, for which one received the spiritual equivalent of the electric chair: Hell. I was polluted with *impure thoughts.* Could I make a clean breast of it, have a heart-to-heart, with Monsignor Hayes, a fuming, red-faced, foul-tempered man whose starched black cassock denied the very existence of genitals?

Thus, once in the Confessional, I repressed (a charitable term in this instance) my sins, typical though they were, because I was too ashamed, too scared, to mention them. I fabricated a generic roster of infractions, threw a reasonable integer next to each, then split with a canned benediction and a canned penance: three Our Fathers and three Hail Marys. *Go in peace and sin no more.*

Like any little Catholic, taught in the 50s and 60s by nuns who beat the shit out of you if you told the truth, I lied. Yet the only way to get my soul snowy white again was to tell the unvarnished truth and be forgiven through the sacrament of Penance. The irony was supreme. Even as I confessed my sins, I sinned, digging a deeper, fierier pit for myself by lying to my Confessor, perjuring my soul: sacrilege.

After a while, my angst and conscience got the better of me. I couldn't take the round-robin of sin atop sin atop sin and then bearing the vaults of guilt that resulted from hoodwinking the priest. I was also anxious about the future, like 1969, when I would have real trespasses to confess. The entire sacrament was a setup, a sucker game. Like a spouse in an abusive marriage, one day I packed what little I could carry and took off. No more confession for me.

It became a small matter to lie to my parents about going to Confession, about attending Mass and receiving the Eucharist. I became a lapsed Catholic, my self-imposed exile resulting ultimately in an unofficial, yet very real, excommunication, not simply the rhetorical kind that Monsignor Hayes doled out when he was in a bad mood—not to mention I ended up marrying, God forbid, a Southern Baptist in Indian Creek Baptist Church in Stone Mountain, Georgia. I never felt good about jumping the sacramental ship all those years ago, but I was trying to survive. It was the only way to salvage my sanity. The stakes were that high. What's more, I've never forsaken Catholicism. Maybe I'm sacrilegiously guilty of attributing a kind of regular-guy-empathy to God, but I remain convinced that He understands.

From where I'm sitting, this moment in Del's, a mere five months from the 21st century, devouring my fiery Chicken Diavolo, I figure even God is cynical of the entire process of Confession. As my pals and I recount our greatest hits of Confession trauma, Father Richard finishes chewing a chicken liver and responds to my question about "piddly, little" sins.

"It doesn't matter whether or not I think what I'm told in the confessional is serious, or even irrelevant. What's important is that the people confessing want to be unburdened of what's troubling them, no matter how big or how small. They want to be forgiven, to be made whole again by God's mercy. My job is simply to listen and be an instrument of that mercy. I can't tell them that they're worried over nothing or to forget about it."

I, and the other lapsed Catholic guys at the table, whose estrangement from Catholicism at least loosely parallels mine, gaze at our buddy who hung in there and became a priest. A good priest. Gentle. Nonjudgmental. The kind one could tell anything without reprisal. *God's mercy.* Not God's wrath. The sacrament of Penance had never been explained by the nuns as existing to make the penitent feel better. I had always thought it was instituted to make one feel worse, to scare and scar so deeply that it did not absolve you of sin, but extorted you of it through ritual degradation. Even our exclusively Protestant wives seem impressed by Father Richard's testimony. They have been listening to our horror stories for years.

We leave Del's, stroll up Liberty Avenue toward the cars, and linger in the sticky shadow of Saint Joe's to chat a little more. On the steep concrete steps leading up to the church vestibule, the guy who had waved to us earlier is passed out, shelved like an invertebrate. It's 1:30 in the morning. Bars are sounding last call. From their doors flash light and clutches of murky conversation as people straggle in and out.

We make our protracted goodbyes, and everybody takes off except for Joan, Phil and I. We cross the street to the gallery, and study the angels in its windows. Joan is instantly arrested by a life-size oil; maybe it's a photograph. Open palms, outstretched arms, its robes whipping about, and the long hair like froth create the illusion of up-swell, ascension. But its eyes are filmed, thrown back in plastery sockets. The angel is blind. From one shoulder its tunic is shorn, exposing a full, decidedly female breast. Its wings drip like lingerie.

Standing behind my wife, her hair turned marble in the avenue's dank industrial light, her dress glowing as she seemingly levitates, I lean against a parking meter and stare at her staring at the angel who stares sightlessly back at us. Pulling on a cigarette, Phil stands next to me, his eyes, too, fixed on Joan and the window.

"Hey, man, can you spare a smoke?"

I turn around and there he is—the guy who had been sprawled on the church steps. Like one of those 60s Bozo Bop Bag punching toys, with the weighted bottoms, he dangerously lists one way and then another, but by some crazy feat of gravity keeps from keeling over. Phil forks over the last cigarette from his pack of Richland Menthols.

The guy asks, "How about one for the road?"

Philip turns the empty pack upside-down and shakes it. "You just got one for the road."

The guy seems amused by this. He smiles, plants a foot that threatens to walk off without him, then asks sheepishly, "Can I get a light?"

Like everything else that night, he's a parody. A parody of a drunk. His words come out in shambling hiccups, slurs and burbles like Crazy Guggenheim from the old *Jackie Gleason Show*. With some difficulty, he finds his mouth with the cigarette. Phil holds up the lighter to it. Staring down his nose at the fire, the guy gets the fantods so badly, Phil can't get the cigarette lit. The guy starts crying. An all out shameless boo-hooing, bubbling sob like some four-time loser in a film noir trying to weasel out of his comeuppance. Embarrassing even for the assassin. *Pow.*

Phil takes back the cigarette, lights it himself, sticks it back in the guy's corrugated mouth, shakes his head and walks into the gallery. He does not suffer drunks well.

"I'm sorry," gurgles the guy, dragging on the cigarette, phlegmily nickering as he tries to compose himself and get his ballast. "It's just… I'm sorry."

"It's okay," I say.

Rumpled, but not cruddy, a half-moon belly above his sagging beltline, he's probably my age, with a thatch of sandy hair and the face of a koala. He looks a tad like W.C. Fields.

"Can you spare a couple bucks?" he asks.

This is inevitable, city life, the point in the narrative where I have been coached to walk away or tell him to get lost. A cigarette is one thing, money another. I sold a few books after the reading, so I have a stash of bills in my pocket. I peel off two ones and hand them to him. Extending his arm to take it, his balance again forsakes him and he begins to capsize. I grab him and stuff the money into his jeans pocket.

"Thanks, man. Thanks."

Then his pupils dilate as if he'd just seen Beelzebub saunter down Liberty Avenue and beckon him. A vision with *TERROR* in bold caps hacks out of his eyeballs.

"Oh, God," he weeps, tears coursing down his face. "I'm sorry. I'm so sorry. I'm bad. I'm so sorry. Oh, God."

"It's okay."

"I am so sorry. I am so bad."

"No, you're not. You're okay."

"Just gimme a hug," he says thick, boozily, as if his mouth is padded with batting. "Can you just gimme a hug?"

As we hug, I am subsumed in his equilibrium, forced to sway along with him. He holds on much too long. On his back I feel through his sweat-soaked shirt the upraised scars where his wings have been amputated. Over his shoulder, I see Joan in the gallery doorsill. She cries softly as she watches our strange dance. Behind her, the blind angel reaches into the Braille night.

A touch of vertigo settles wetly over me. He won't let go, and I want him off me. My city instincts flash. What the hell am I doing? Almost two in the morning, hugging a vagrant inebriated out of his mind. Suddenly I'm a little panicky, ready to pop him if I have to. But he's still sobbing, "I'm sorry" over and over, and I peel him off me as gently as I can. Joan has vanished into the gallery.

"I want to sit down. I just want to sit down."

I muscle him over to a cafe stoop, ease him down, and prop him against a wall.

"I'm sorry. Oh, God, I'm so sorry," his sobs subsiding into whispery soughs.

"It's okay. You didn't do anything," I absolve him one last time, but elect not to hit him with a penance. He's already saddled with a ponderous one.

By now he is exhausted, like a child, in his ineffable desperate contrition, who has cried too much, too long, and has no idea what is really wrong or how to fix it. He is in a swoon by the time he tilts to the concrete floor. I add a ten spot to the singles already in his pocket. Good money atop bad. Twelve dollars down the drain. What the hell. You can't get much of a meal or much of a drunk on a couple bucks.

Not only that. The money I abandon to his pocket amounts to both alms and payoff, the amortization of guilt. Because he is the dispossessed, heartsick, homeless derelict in the street, I am not. At least this is the way I have come to conceive of it. My savior, he suffers in my place. I love him even as I fear him. At the very least, I must forgive him. Twelve dollars seems cheap to keep him in the gutter instead of me.

Joining Joan and Phil in the stifling gallery, I shamble around looking at the art. On the wall just behind the podium hangs a huge smoky blue oil of the Blessed Mother's head. Superimposed over her left eye is a gossamer, pale yellow square. Before the reading, two nuns paused before it. I overheard their discussion: they had fixed upon the yellow square as symbolic of Mary's inner light—which was completely satisfactory, though a touch oversimplified. But I couldn't come up with anything better.

After the reading, during question and answer, one of the nuns asked me why I write. A dreaded question, really. I don't know that writers often think consciously of their motives; the answer lies inscrutably imbedded in their work. In responding to such a question, there exists also the potential to make a pedantic fool of oneself, especially with one's entire perspiring family looking on. Leave it to a nun.

A few years ago, I was in the mountain town of Asheville, North Carolina and walked into the beautiful cathedral of Saint Lawrence, situated portentously on a shimmering hill. It was Saturday afternoon. Outside each confessional queued the penitents. With fear and hesitation, I shuffled into one of the lines. When it was my turn, I planned to kneel down in that box and say, "Bless me, Father, for I have sinned. My last confession was thirty-one years ago." Then I was going to spill, no holds barred, take my medicine, and emerge with a sparkling soul.

But the line moved slowly and I had to be somewhere soon. Not with small relief, I hustled out of the cathedral. Despite my considerable education—what I regard as my own well thought out spiritual evolution, and my worldliness—the confessional and the thought of confession still traumatize me.

Nevertheless, I wanted desperately to be forgiven, and it appears I require a ritual, a sacrament, to accomplish it.

My response to the nun's question surprised me: that I write because it affords me a chance to be a better person, to see and speak the *truth* that is perhaps invisible during the actual experience I'm writing about. "I write," I confessed, "to be forgiven."

And there it is. Perhaps what everybody is searching for. Another chance. Regeneration. Forgiveness. What Father Richard termed "God's Mercy." Isn't confession central to the human spirit? Perhaps in *telling* the story of our transgressions, we obtain, at least subconsciously, forgiveness—and can go on.

Who knows? I can't look at angels any more. I especially can't take the gallery's heat. The three of us walk back outside. The drunk guy is gone. Disappeared into the pitiless city. Traffic has picked up dramatically. Cars zip out of alleys and side streets and flood the avenue. The sidewalks crowd with people.

"What's up?" I say to Phil.

"Bars just closed."

Everywhere throughout Pittsburgh, in every city and town on Eastern Standard time, people who have spent the night in bars, drinking too much, take to the highway. And all but a handful make it home.

Busboy

The first real job I had was bussing tables at Sodini's, a fashionable restaurant in the Squirrel Hill section of Pittsburgh. It sat at the apex of Wilkins Avenue, not far from its intersection with Beechwood Boulevard's a promenade of cinematic beeches and swooning mansions, in one of which resided *the* Mr. Rogers. In his storybook neighborhood, it was always a beautiful day.

Squirrel Hill, wealthy, foreign, seductive, was the Jewish enclave of the city. For some reason, when my sister and I were small children, my parents carted us there to purchase our church shoes at Sims on Forbes Avenue; and, for a stretch, my mother, an itinerant, expert seamstress, worked in the tailor shop at Sol Mentz's, a men's clothing store, also on Forbes. On Friday evenings, the Hassidic Jewish men, in wide black hats, black foreboding frock coats and furious Old Testament beards, trudged along the sidewalks with Sabbath groceries.

The summer of 1971, I was 17 years old, soon to be 18, spending my last months home before packing off to my freshman year at California State College, an outpost in the coal-rife Monongahela Valley not far from the borders of Ohio and West Virginia. I had applied there only because a friend applied. I had also figured, without a bit of investigation, that California was ideally gauged to my latent talents: athletically and intellectually. More than anything, I aimed to play football there.

I didn't want the job at Sodini's, or any job, but it was offered to me in front of my parents, by my predecessor, a neighbor, who had to leave early for his senior year at Purdue. To refuse would have been to acknowledge my true mettle which, I suppose, was not much. My parents, fierce unionists, a seamstress and a steelworker, were children of early 20th century Italian immigrants—a population pathologically dedicated to assimilation. Sisyphean toil existed in their minds as privilege, sacrosanct as the true cross—as if bereft of backbreaking, even demeaning, labor, one could never hope to enter the Kingdom. The precise tally of men and women was calculated by how many hours they kept their shoulders to the wheel. That I assign my parents' working class aesthetic to allegory is a measure of how very seriously employment, and worthwhile industry of any pedigree—work, by God, *work*—was looked upon in our home, and in my extended family on both sides. You did not trifle when it came to work, and a wage-earning job was nothing short of sacramental.

That I did not want to work was perhaps the only thing I really knew about myself that summer. While I had enjoyed a competent, though undistinguished, career as a high school football player, I had decided I wanted to play at the small college I was about to enter—even though I had not been recruited. I had written an impassioned letter declaring my intentions to the head football coach there. I reasoned not only that such letters were answered, but that the response to my pluck would be not merely an invitation to try out, but a full scholarship.

I don't think for a minute that I ever truly thought I'd play college football. It was a pleasing little lie I told myself. I was attempting to hold on to an identity, a mythologized self, which had never actually existed. What I was most concerned with that summer was growing my hair to an exaggerated length. I wanted it as long as possible, so that when I appeared for the first time as a student on a college campus, there would be no doubt as to my advanced state of consciousness. In addition, I was cultivating a little mustache which I was sure would any day blossom into the lush Joe Namath-like Fu Manchu I so desperately desired. Every morning, however, smirking back at me from my upper lip in the bathroom mirror were the sparse black tendrils of a pimp.

The day before I started my job at Sodini's, I went in to talk to the restaurant owner. Mr. Sodini was a big-bellied, thick-limbed older Italian man with a thatch of white hair and an implacable, leathery self-assuredness—like he'd allow you to break brick after brick across his gargantuan Roman nose before he good-naturedly squashed you with one of his club-like hands. The first thing he told me was that I'd have to get a haircut. This was a terrific blow. I hated the job already. How in the world could I proclaim my otherness without long hair? The shock must have registered on my face.

"You don't mind getting a haircut, do you?"

"No, Sir," I lied.

"Good. You need to wear a necktie too. You got a necktie?"

"Yes, Sir."

We shook hands. He lumbered off through two swinging aluminum doors, each with a glass porthole at eye level, leading into the kitchen. I inked in a few forms, slumped off to Sam DeRoss's Barber Shop, a place I had figured to never visit again, and left the better part of my identity on his scuffed tile floor. Thank God, I still had my mustache.

When I showed up at Sodini's for my shift the next day, with a high and tight hairdo, I was given over to apprentice under a kid named Tommy, a few years older than I. His dad, Big Tommy, was one of the chefs. Tommy was the Foghorn Leghorn, *Let me show you how it's done, Son,* of busboys. A wiry little guy with a prow of slicked black hair and a constant burning butt dangling from his mouth. The top-kick of bussing, his white Nehru bus-jacket was pressed and starched. Rigged out in my own bus-jacket, and oozing mediocrity, I felt like a porter, or one of those guys who wheel gurneys around the morgue.

With a flourish, Tommy led me into the kitchen to introduce me to everyone. Tommy's dad, the only chef who seemed to speak English, greeted me warmly. The others, Italians, smiled and waved ladles and whisks. Their white, billowing mushroom hats listed in the steam rising from the delicious-smelling pots and saucepans. There was also the dishwasher—I can't remember his name—a big, smiling, very fat black man with his arms up to his biceps in a foaming slop sink. Of the several waitresses, I can only remember Mabel and Stella, seasoned veterans, no doubt, who had been through countless campaigns. Mabel was a dead ringer for blonde actor Rose Marie who played the endearing wiseacre Sally on *The Dick Van Dyke Show*. Stella was a bowling ball, Italian as *pasta fagolio*, no nonsense, pencil behind an ear, a fullback with an apron and hairnet. She had lived through plenty of busboys.

Tommy and I shared the prep work: topped salt and pepper shakers, ketchup bottles, and sugar bowls; bundled silverware in cloth napkins; made sure each table had a fresh tablecloth, full setups, clean ashtrays and a lit hurricane lamp. We paused, in the cellar, before carrying cases of beer and wine and sodas up, to each drink, at Tommy's urging, a warm Heineken. He knew the ropes, and in the world of pro bussing such liberties were expected.

When it came time to vacuum, Tommy, claiming he had something to do, disappeared into the kitchen, a place which, for him, seemed to serve the same function within the restaurant that the Sacristy does in the church: a kind of *For Members Only* club, clearly not for the unanointed. This irritated me—this sudden division of labor, this relegation. I had never in my life pushed a vacuum cleaner. But I had been alive long enough to know about pecking orders and, over the years, had certainly benefited from them. Even so, as I bulled the unwieldy industrial Hoover over the dining room's garish floral carpet, among the tables and chairs, then on into the bar where a few patrons, not noticing me in the least, had already gathered to drink before dinner, I found myself faced with my own insignificance. Even worse was the fact that, in the hierarchy of that restaurant, I was at dead bottom, the dishwasher notwithstanding. At least he was able to suffer in private and, should he desire, grow his hair to the floor.

It wasn't that I thought I was too good for the work. Rather it was my singular anonymity that disheartened me. I was not too good to suction grime out of an institutional carpet. I was simply too good. Period. Why should these people in Sodini's bar—dressed in the casual opulence of people who arrive by yacht—be eating and drinking and enjoying themselves while I, their humble shit-eating servant, made sure they could drink their Tom Collinses and Manhattans in glittering, candlelit, red leather grottos?

I became outraged. There wasn't a blessed thing in what I was doing as a busboy that reflected who I really was. To those pampered diners, I was nothing more than 150 pounds of blood and bone, gristle and guts who could wield a vacuum cleaner and manhandle befouled tableware from one place to another. None of them knew that only a day before I had had hair down to my shoulders; that I had a pretty girlfriend who was wild about me; that I had led my high school football team in interceptions (2); that I was headed for college on, maybe, a football scholarship and, come autumn, wearing the red and black of the California State College Vulcans, I'd be on the gridiron, surveying the world through a double bar and bull-ring; that I was on a bee-line for fame as a swashbuckling trial lawyer who could buy and sell them a hundred times over. I was a Vulcan, damn it, not some pituitary houseboy.

That an almost-eighteen year old boy lives more thoroughly in the flesh than in the spirit is no revelation. I suppose I half expected those chic, sleek people in that bar to recognize me for the rarified human I was and invite me to join their party. That this didn't happen threw me for a loop. My delusions of grandeur, my superiority, were exploded. I was like everyone else. Only less.

After vacuuming I had about fifteen minutes to eat before the front doors were unlocked and the dining room opened. Employees were permitted certain items, gratis, off the menu. My meal never varied: ravioli, a hot fudge sundae and a glass of milk. In a stupor, at a little table in a corner of the torrid kitchen, I'd eat this scrumptious, familiar food, imagining myself elsewhere, as I listened simultaneously to the dishwasher sing David Ruffin while *La Traviata* mewled on the staticky kitchen radio.

There is a certain drama that attends the moment when a restaurant actually swings open its front doors and customers march in: a bit like opening night in the theatre, and with the same self-conscious gravity. Mr. Sodini would storm into the kitchen wearing an expensive suit, taste a few of the sauces, make sure the wine temperatures were perfect, then stride into the dining room to charm his pet customers. The chefs stopped smiling, became petulant and artistic. Armed with their pads, and trays like medieval shields, the waitresses queued just inside the kitchen doors, Tommy and I like footmen just behind them. With a twenty minute cushion before the first avalanche of dirty dishes, the dishwasher, smiling and smoking one cigarette after another, sat like Gotama on a five gallon bucket of detergent.

Once the evening ignited in earnest, I never stopped running. My job was to put the dirty china, glasses and cutlery into a grey rubber tub on a stainless steel cart, empty the ashtrays, grab the tips and put them in the appropriate waitress's jar, strip the table, mop it with a wet rag, set up the table, bust through the treacherous swinging doors into the kitchen, set the tub on the table next to the dishwasher's sink, grab a clean tub, and then double-time back to the dining room and do it again.

There was no variation, just Tommy and I tearing around and the waitresses humping those giant trays, two trays sometimes, hammering through the silver doors, looking crazed like doped horses in the last furlong, eyes rheumy, even nostalgic—like we were in something pretty damned dire together—everything about them threatening us to step up the pace, that this was no joke, but do-or-die livelihood. What my parents were always testifying about. All the while, Mr. Sodini waltzed among the tables, glad-handing, a lugubrious Sicilian smile chiseled into his jaw.

I liked this part of the job: the frantic, sweating sprint. It was exciting. Sometimes, Tommy would look at me in the middle of it as if to say, *Ain't this bussing some serious tough guy shit?* I hustled to stay a step ahead, not because I had any interest in the job, but because I was trying to beat something. I figured I could do anything Tommy could do. It was my left-handed way of retaining my integrity. Maybe it was my one-Heineken buzz.

At the end of the night, after Tommy and I had dragged the last pan of crud into the dishwasher, still smiling, sweating buckets, ostensibly enjoying his nightly scald and sauna for which he was paid who knows how little; after we had set up for the next day's lunch, bagged the trash and threw it in the dumpster; after I had lugged the hateful Hoover back up the cellar steps to vacuum again as Tommy retreated for his mysterious assignation in the kitchen, there was one last chore—without question, my favorite.

Tommy and I took all of the empty booze, soft drink, and various other bottles out to the sultry, summer parking lot behind the kitchen and smashed them in an empty 55 gallon drum stationed in a grove of dwarfed Sumacs. There were so many empties that to cart them off intact we would have needed a truck. In shivers, however, they fit nicely inside the barrel. The first one, *smash*; then the next and the next, *smash, smash, smash*, each of us jockeying for the green champagne mags and the big Chivas Regal empties; they made the biggest explosions. Then the remainder of the top shelf: J&B, Dewars, Cutty Sark, Courvoisier, Finlandia, Wild Turkey. Followed by the infantry—a battalion of beer and pop and Perrier bottles.

Fifteen minutes of smashing frenzy that left us giddy—somehow I felt vindicated—and the drum brimmed with luminous broken glass. Then we sat down with the dishwasher on the concrete steps leading out of the kitchen, smoked a cigarette and punched out.

I'd take off for my girl's where I'd lay out to her how exploited I felt. She'd stroke my bristly head, compliment my mustache and tell me that I was still pretty cool, that I could take that bunch of high class diners with one hand tied behind me. While I cultivated a decided contempt for those diners, they afforded me a glimpse into a life that I began to think might be worth living. They had a practiced *savoir faire*, their manners were impeccable, if a tad condescending, and they ate the most heavenly food. My chief source of resentment was not at the menial nature of the tasks I performed at the restaurant, but over the fact that in their eyes I was invisible. How was I so easy to ignore? Why didn't they recognize in me a comrade, a *bon vivante*, a fellow who would add even more luster to their golden lives? Why didn't they insist that I forsake my nasty bus tub and join them for Cherrystone Clams, Oysters Rockefeller, Veal Marsala, Crab Devonshire, Filet Mignon, Dom Perignon, Chocolate Mousse, a discreet Drambuie? I lusted after their food; the splendor of it dilated my synapses. I went so far as to cadge it from their plates as I cleaned up; and later in the secrecy of the basement, as I fetched my darling Hoover, I chewed and swallowed what they had been too full to eat.

One night, as I was bussing a table, I looked up and saw a boy I'll call Paul DiLeo, Hollywood handsome, with long black hair, sitting at an adjacent table with a crew of young men and women my age, feasting on the very food, only a few days before, I had known neither existed nor could have pronounced. They formed such a tableau of aching perfection that I almost wept. One thing I hadn't bargained for was seeing at Sodini's anyone who knew me. My neighborhood, though not many miles off, was aesthetically in another country. Paul, who came from a wealthy family that owned a prominent Pittsburgh business, had gone to a rival high school. He and I had first met on a wrestling mat pitted against each other. I had beaten him, barely, 2-1. That mere point was the lording margin over him I planned to take to my grave. Occasionally we'd see each other at dances and parties and, though we never spoke about the match, I knew and he knew what had happened between us that winter night, two years before, in an ancient overheated Catholic gym.

Seeing me in my white coat, rag in hand, he smiled and waved; and in that instant my winning point not only fell away, but dipped into the negatives until I was badly shutout, decimated, pinned in the first period. Feeling like an organ grinder's monkey, I wanted to storm his table and smash everything, but all I could do was wave back at all those beautiful people. My compromise was complete.

On my sixth evening at the restaurant, I sat by myself in the cellar drinking my tepid bottle of beer and staring at the vacuum cleaner. I wondered when that college football coach was going to answer my letter. Every night, after arriving home from work, I sifted anxiously through the mail for my scholarship offer. Summer practice was due to start in about a week—my ticket out of the world of bussing into the world of glitter and notoriety, my inevitable due.

I stashed the empty Heineken and reached for the vacuum cleaner. I jerked my hand back—like I had been cut or burnt. Then I saw the lone wasp limping along the handle. I knocked it off and eviscerated it under my shoe. My hand hurt like hell, but it wasn't just the pain. It was the accretion of indignities that that brilliant, infinitesimal, yet exponential, sting represented. Tears of fury filled my eyes. I grabbed the Hoover and bolted up the steps.

As I went by the kitchen doors, Stella, barreling out with a loaded tray for the bar, literally knocked me down. Standing over me, not saying a word, she looked at me as if I were the stupidest, sorriest annoyance she had ever seen. I was out of my mind with anger, way too far gone to let things go, humiliated enough to bite her. I jumped to my feet. I can't say what exactly happened, though I have documented in my memory a vision of Stella and I going at it toe to toe like a couple of street-fighters. I want to say that she promptly busted me in the mouth with her fist, that I then reached back and popped her in the head—she had a solid eighty pounds on me—that we stood there for a long time slugging. Undoubtedly this did not happen. I was not raised to fistfight with women, especially those who could handily kick my ass. Nevertheless, in the ensuing melee, the tray of food she'd been toting crashed to the floor. Devonshire splattered on her black nurse's shoes. Mabel pulled me away, saying, "It's alright, honey," while it took a couple of chefs to restrain Stella.

I had to clean everything up; it was my job anyhow. I apologized and Stella and I shook hands. I figured Mr. Sodini would fire me, but no one seemed all that worked up about what had happened. Apparently that kind of thing can jump off in high stakes restaurant work.

It was difficult eating my ravioli that night. Maybe my jaw felt broken from the imagined sucker punch Stella laid on me. In reality, I was just having trouble swallowing—a symptom of folks afflicted with hubris—as I wolfed not exactly the first unsavory plate of humility I'd ingest in the world of wages.

What is true, not a whit of license, before God, I swear, is that after I finished my sundae, I called home from a phone in the cellar. My mother answered. She was the enforcer, the parent you didn't want to trifle with. My dad was an even, totally reasonable, guy. But they were both maniacs when it came to punching a time clock. I asked her if I could quit the job at Sodini's. My mother did not summon my dad or ask his opinion or insist I talk it over with him. He would not have known what to say. Like my mother, however, he would have surely been dismayed that he had raised a son with so little regard for an honest day's work. My mother must have told me it was okay. I'm sure I sounded pitiful. What would I have said to her? That I was worthless? That I had been stung by a bee? That I thought maybe I had brawled, in the middle of the restaurant, with a middle-aged waitress? I know for certain that I did not confide my shame.

When I got off the phone, I went to Mr. Sodini's office and told him that I had to quit the job: my mother had just informed me in a telephone conversation that in that day's mail a letter had miraculously come from the football coach at California State College, and I had been offered a full scholarship to play there. Summer practice started in a week, so I had loose ends to tie up.

He came out from around his desk and shook my hand. "That's wonderful. I'm proud of you."

"Thank you, Mr. Sodini."

"We'll miss you. You've been doing a good job here. I hope you'll come back and see us."

I assured him I would. We shook hands again. Then I went back to work out the last hours of my six-day abbreviated bussing career. All told, I ended up making about sixty bucks. I had also endured for nothing the ignominy of a haircut, and was obliged to admit to my anxious, crestfallen parents that I had not inherited from them and my forbears the drop of gumption necessary to make it in the world as a busboy—not even for a lousy week.

There was nothing about that job I ever missed. Except shattering those bottles in the rusted steel drum at the end of the night, lethal shards glinting as they sprayed the hot black moonlit sky, the glow of Sodini's kitchen spilling into the parking lot, the distant lament of opera and the dishwasher's hulking silhouette as he pulled on a cigarette in the open doorway. Perhaps what I valued about this ritual was its kinship with vandalism: breaking bottles, breaking windows. Perhaps I had unwittingly placed too much of a premium on breaking. I'd have to walk that jagged glass for the rest of my life.

Ghostwriting

Bull City looks like Fidel Castro: green yard bird fatigues, engineer's cap and a mule-tail, anarchist beard. He's from Missoula, Montana, but took his fall, a life sentence, in Wilkes County, pretty tough cowboy country, 45 minutes up the road. His moonshine and mesquite accent rolls out of cave-rock. He carries into the creative writing class I'm teaching at the Iredell County Prison, in Statesville, North Carolina, a Bible, a dictionary, chain gang loose-leaf, and two sharpened pencils. He aims to be a writer.

If asked, Bull City would say he's simply making his time, being a man. He works a gained-time job at the prison's furniture factory, learning a trade he can put to use if he ever gets out. The job and his writing and the Lord keep him busy, though not in that order. The Lord comes first, he is fast to stipulate. I'd wager he's in for murder. Crime of passion. While the free world sees murderers at the bottom of the criminal sump, thanks to the media who demonize them all as axe-wielding serial killers, that particular pedigree on the yard is really its most honorable, affable and predictable. A tiny percentage of men and woman sent up for murder recidivate; the insane, emotionally-charged circumstances that land them in prison are highly stylized, and tend to never duplicate themselves.

But Bull City could have done anything: set fire to a town or poisoned a reservoir. Booze, guns, and drugs shadow his eyes, scars and tattoos. More to the point, you can't glean a thing about a man by just looking at him—especially in prison, where discussing crime stories is strictly taboo. What he's done doesn't matter. For certain, he's brushed up against the beast and come away with that cauterized long-time felon stare. The sorrow of his past has made him vulnerable enough to turn to God, and grow into a strong and serious prisoner. One can plainly see that no one, guard nor inmate, would willingly interfere with him.

The first sentence of his story is memorable: "With routine grace, the sun rises." Then his inmate protagonist wakes from restive slumber, as so many of these stories begin, and hits the yard. It's early. The moon still hangs over the wire. Right away he sees that something's wrong. The whole rhythm of the joint is about two notches grimmer, guys full of fear and loathing, a few in tears. He makes inquiries and discovers that during the night something happened to Forty-four, a sweet, righteous dude. Everyone's favorite. Solid, never up in your business, but comforting when you need him. Not with his mouth, but simply by being on the set. An aces guy all around.

The story sounds reasonable. In here, in this classroom, they all do; but if you look away for a moment, assess your surroundings—the pallor and bloodshot eyes, the astringent smell of fear and custody, a guard peeping in every so often, the razory shoulders of wire visible through the Ed Building window—you might figure it's the worst kind of made-up, a con, a come-on, and that you are in danger. You have to sit back like it's nothing, like there's not a thing in the world you'd be shocked by. The men you sit in the room with could kill you.

The other guys stare faithfully at Bull City as he reads. He loved Forty-four. His voice is deep and sure, and he's not turning away from what's in his heart. What you'd expect from

Montana. He looks up occasionally to catch the eyes of his audience as they nod. They know this story. Forty-four was their partner too. Many of them figure into the story. The stakes are high. I realize that Bull City is recounting something that really happened.

His piece has little of the trumped-up rhetoric, the wordiness and melodrama, that so often characterizes prison writing. Both in its flat declarative style, and its plot and pacing, the story is gripping, far far better than the usual beginning inmate writing, which tends toward the sensational. The conflict is palpable. I'm truly intrigued with Forty-four; I want to know what happened to him. What really sets Bull City's writing apart is its lack of swagger and defiance. There's a tenderness to this story usually lacking in prison writing. Not to say that tenderness isn't regularly broached: the lament for the ubiquitous chain gang Penelope left back in the streets, her soothing caress, yearning for a brood of darling babies. Images of what a straight life outside the penitentiary might be like. But the writing tends on the first go-round to be predictable, derivative, most often over-sentimentalized—not so dissimilar, really, to first stabs in any creative writing classroom. In this instance, what ends up mattering more than anything is that these convicts have willingly entered this room. Period. From where they are sitting, merely showing up for this class, taught by a complete stranger, some white guy in a necktie who teach-es at the local college, is a harrowing leap.

The guys in Bull City's story set out to look for Forty-four. They comb every inch of the cellblock and the yard. Nothing. Not a trace. But they don't want to ask the yard man because Forty-Four might have run and they don't want to tip the guards. But to just split like this? They have a bad feeling. The south tower guard, just coming off first shift, notices them congregated and asks what's up. *Nothing*, they tell him. *Not a goddam thing.* He leads them back to the quarry fence. There's Forty-four, twelve feet in the air, dangling in bloody coils of concertina.

Forty-four had tried to escape, got hooked in the wire and the guard left him up there all night to bleed to death. It's not a true story after all. In this context, of course, the guards are the bad guys—everyone in class agrees on this—but in real life they just couldn't get away with this: ignoring a skewered escape cut to pieces in the concertina. But it doesn't have to be true. This is, after all, creative writing. Not bad. Not terribly unpredictable; but, again, Bull City doesn't turn away from his grief and unapologetic love for Forty-four. That's a breakthrough, the kind of honesty a writer must aspire to. I glance about the room. The other guys are right there with him. They are down with this story in a way I don't really apprehend. Turmoil is mapped on their faces as Bull City moves to the true denouement.

The night before, at lockdown, under a full moon, an owl had swooped into the yard and snatched Forty-four. *Wow*, I think. But the owl, with the weight of Forty-four in his talons, hadn't had the lift to clear the fence and Forty-four snagged in the concertina. What an image. Bull City then reveals that Forty-four is a rabbit—what the other guys in the room have known all along. A rabbit! *Wow*, I think again; so it is a true story. The tower guard had witnessed the whole thing, watched the snared rabbit writhe in the razors until he expired. The owl had circled until Forty-four was still and then flew off. The guard told the guys that he didn't think Forty-four had suffered much, that he had liked the little guy himself. Then he opened the maintenance shack so they could get a ladder and fetch him down. Which is where the story should have ended. I can't exactly remember how Bull City ended it, but it was long after he should have, after he ended up telling the audience what he wanted them to feel—even though he had already so master-fully and cinematically drilled that image of loss and heartbreak and violence into them: Forty-four trussed in the silver wire and bloody moonlight up there on the fence like a rabbit Messiah.

A beginner's error, easily fixed. I hold my tongue. In prison there are certain stories you simply do not criticize; to do so would be an epic breach of etiquette. Disrespect. Like you didn't get it. Your credibility as a teacher, paradoxically enough, would be ruined. The real permission to enter a prison and teach writing comes not from the prison administration, but from the prisoners themselves. When a man stands there, with it all hanging out, you don't tell him there is a better way to do it. What's more, in telling this story, and telling it well, as evidenced by the moved convict faces I find myself surrounded by, Bull City, for the time being, has become a shaman. He has created among his brethren, the only ones in a position to understand, a sacred space. It isn't the writing, the language, which moved them, but the story itself, that shared sense of loss and longing—their secret terrible power—symbolized in Forty-four.

We do get around to discussing the story. Not craft and such, but the story as communal property. They all knew and loved the real Forty-four. Most important, however, is that he loved them. He didn't care that they were outlaws, the despised lowlife of society. Several of the men contribute remembrances about feeding him, petting him, his absolute trust and constancy, his wisdom. Tender remarks they might utter about family and friends, sentences the free world does not ascribe to prison inmates. Geniuses of failure. Men who have consistently made messes of their lives. Who have been cruel and cavalier and stupid. Yet they have transferred their affections to a little rabbit, sublimated the feelings they have all their lives denied and been denied, trying to do better, to be forgiven. We take a few minutes to eulogize Forty-four. If any of the guys say anything about the writing itself, it's usually something fairly generic like, "I like the way he did that" or simply "I liked it" or "That was good."

The story for them defines something about their plights as prisoners. The sagacious old freedom angel, a bird of prey, no less, came down to rescue Forty-four, but the ballast of time and the pull of the yard were too ponderous. Like Icarus, flying was too much for him. Old Forty-four. Only way to quit the chain gang is to perish. He probably would not have made it on the outside anyhow; that owl was fixing to eat him.

It's not stretching things to say that Bull City's story is a parable, though we don't broach that subject. I'm quick to tell my prison students that I'm not a guard and I'm not a shrink. A prison writing teacher's main job is asking for the story and then listening. You can't really get around to discussing the actual writing (language, trope, narrative strategy, etc.), if ever you do, until you've discussed the story. There's got to be a plot, though their own lives, in actuality, tend toward the surreal—metafiction. For the prisoner, getting it out, like *getting out*, is the highest form of art. Each thinks his story is immortal—not unlike the rest of us.

Many prisoners desire to write because they are certain they have in them a bestseller, a movie. They watch plenty of

TV and know what it takes. Each year I get a handful of letters from inmates imploring me to ghostwrite their blockbusters. Unbelievable stuff, they insist. Sure to sell. We'll split fifty-fifty. No doubt, actually, that in the right hands their stories could bust the block. Their rap sheets alone are page-turners.

At any rate, there's a tacit understanding between teacher and students—not a realistic one—that these classes, all this writing and subsequent discussion, are in the service of being released from the penitentiary. Which, in a very practical sense, isn't true. They will not be released because of their stories. In all likelihood, their stories might inhibit their release. But stories are not practical in the same way that hoping is not practical, yet who can live without either. *Release* is a word of sweeping valence, and writing provides *release* beyond secular freedom. I don't mean *getting in touch* with themselves. They don't need pencils in their hands to afford them introspection. It's the ritual of writing—the confessional, egocentric catharsis of it—that consoles them—that consoles anyone who writes. But they, *offenders*—in much more direct, ritualized ways than free men—desire forgiveness. To be *released.* And writing does work for a while, at least during the workshop, and hopefully on the yard and in the cellblock and, who knows, maybe even beyond the walls. By listening, by nodding in that solemn, funereal way that prisoners nod when one of them is reading his story, they absolve each other. Writing is a place where they can be good and get away with it.

One frigid winter night I taught a poetry workshop deep in one of the sub-cellars of Central Prison, North Carolina's 19th century maximum security penitentiary in Raleigh. Teaching with me was Becky Gould Gibson, a poet friend of mine, a retired English professor at a small Quaker college. It was the first time she had ever been in a prison, and she was much taken with the men—dire felons pulling interminable time for unthinkable atrocities—mystified by their complicated, disastrous lives and moved by their writing. Fearless, elegant, she told them she wanted to feed them poems. Deeply into it, the men opened up. Something extraordinary, religious, occurred—not unusual in a prison writing class—though it was Becky, strolling blithely like a saint into a leper colony, who effected the transformation. For two hours, she and I saw the very best of them. By her lights, they were good men, worthy of another crack at life outside.

As we were leaving, she asked the program officer who had arranged our visit if "parole boards listen to poems?" When he realized that she was completely serious, he told her politely that they did not. Knowing what I know of parole boards, I had the wonderfully absurd vision of inmates winning release by whipping out their poems and evangelizing a stony panel of parole officials.

In his *Confessions*, Saint Augustine writes: "What is more monstrous than to claim that things become better by losing all their good? Therefore, if they are deprived of all good, they will be absolutely nothing." Prisoner writing, even when about the most hideous things, is a personal declaration of vestigial goodness. Goodness denied them, which they of necessity have denied possessing. Writing is their confession of goodness. In an amazing letter to me, one of my students in the *outside* world summed it up best: "I was trying to write like the somebody that I sometimes want to be—you know, the somebody who is me, only better." But this is an abstraction, and inmates don't consciously traffic in abstractions. Make no mistake; they want out.

I have my own confession to make. When I first heard the story of Forty-four, I swore that I would not steal it. It belonged to Bull City and was his to tell. He recognized Forty-four's assignation with that owl as a mystery that could only be related as a story—which took some savvy and decided courage on his part. Not only that. He formalized it in written language. Which made it immortal.

That writers have larcenous hearts is not news. They cannibalize everything, and there's no better trove for such kleptomania than a prison yard. I've known inmates to eat tree bark, howl at the moon, stuff pillows under their shirts so they wouldn't get sliced while climbing through concertina, hack themselves to flinders with razors, keep copperheads as pets, swallow stick deodorant for a buzz, sever an Achilles tendon with a bushaxe on caprice, store film canisters of dope in their rectums, become transsexuals and wear lingerie in the cellblock, vomit baggies of cocaine, fix voodoo dolls on one another and guards. The list is endless and rich and no writer could resist theft—things I have witnessed or heard about or, who knows, imagined. They weren't *written*: what the word becomes when it is inscribed.

But that image, that incomparable, unimaginable, allegorical, filmic image of the owl plucking up the rabbit who is then hideously snared by the concertina (prison's most sanguine symbol) and left to die an agonizing, lonely death was too much to resist. How could I not tell you about it? And if I hadn't—and this is my rationalization—I don't know that it would have ever made it out of prison. Like Bull City, like the rabbit Forty-four, it would have simply done life to die; and it is too amazing a story to remain forever, like all the other stories doing dark and silent time, behind concertina. Though I recount it, there is no way I can claim it for my own. I'm not sure I understand it. While I have an everyman's empathy for these men and their stories, I'm only the ghostwriter. Every day, on the road, I see dead rabbits.

Real Work

All the sons of the Church should remember that their exalted status is to be attributed not to their own merits but to the special grace of Christ.

The Dogmatic Constitution on the Church
(Lumen Gentium)

"We should be mixing cement on some open plain ..."
—Biff from *Death of a Salesman*
—Arthur Miller

The summer of 1976, the bicentennial year—the year I left my home town of Pittsburgh for good to trek to North Carolina to work in a prison as a VISTA Volunteer—I was employed as a laborer, a hod carrier to be precise, for my Uncle Leo, one of my mother's brothers, a successful, wealthy brick contractor. A millionaire, the family whispered. My pay was $2.75 an hour, by far the highest wage I had ever earned.

On my VISTA application, I had pinpointed Montana as my number one choice for a gig—simply because Montana struck me as a grand and unfathomable. However, because I fit the *generalist* rubric—meaning that unlike plumbers, nurses, electricians, physicians, etc., I had no specific skill in anything—I fetched an assignment at Huntersville Prison, in deep country, twelve miles north of Charlotte.

I had applied to VISTA not because I knew what I wanted to do, but because the list of what I couldn't stomach doing was so ponderously long. Smoldering in me, as well, was the desire to leave Pittsburgh. Not because I felt trapped or nursed a grudge against it—on the contrary—but because I was sure that leaving was the right thing you do. As if I had received a spiritual imprimatur. Had I been rejected by VISTA, my friend David Friday and I planned to buy brand new Harleys, throttle them cross-country to California, sell them there in the Golden State for a grubstake and see what happened. I also had half a dozen law school applications stacked on my bedroom desk—from places like Yale, Dickinson, Suffolk, and Tufts—that made my mother salivate.

That summer I was also taking my last three hours of course work one evening a week toward completion of a Master's degree in English Literature from the University of Pittsburgh where I had a mere twelve months earlier completed my undergraduate degree in English Literature. The class was Latin American Literature, taught by Harry Mooney, my advisor, the high priest of literature, "the knight of the rueful figure," whom I idolized. He was a graduate in 1951 of Pittsburgh Central Catholic High School—three blocks away from Pitt on the same street, Fifth Avenue—where I had also graduated, twenty years after Dr. Mooney, in 1971.

In 1976, Latin American Literature was esoteric. The world had not yet been hyphenated. My family was still Italian, though soon, without realizing it, we would become Italian-Americans, a benefit I'm still not sure I've realized. I had never heard of the canonical Latin American writers: Gabriel Garcia Marquez, Jorge Luis Borges, Julio Cortazar, Carlos Fuentes, Manuel Puig et al.—household literary names these days. Until that course, no one had told me *One Hundred Years of Solitude*, which I had never heard of either—the novel was a mere nine years old at the time—was considered by many the greatest novel of the twentieth century. I was three credits shy of a Master's Degree in Literature and I had never heard of the greatest novel of the 20th century. That was just the tip of the iceberg of my ignorance.

Prior to laboring for my uncle, I had been fired from my previous two jobs: driving a delivery truck for a flower shop, and as a drone at a toy warehouse. The jobs I had had prior to those positions, I had quit, or perhaps been fired (the distinction was ever-blurring back then): as a night-watchman at an apartment building, and as a busboy. By the summer of '76, I had decided I wanted to be a writer. But of course I hadn't known what that was, what it entailed, how you arranged to be one. I had taken one undergraduate creative writing class at Pitt—Advanced Poetry Workshop—and emerged from it with a sheaf of benighted verse that my professor, Ed Ochester, an important American poet, had been very kind about, though I imagine him alone in his office rolling his eyes over it, and perhaps even reading a couplet or two of it aloud to his colleagues, my other professors, just for laughs. Nevertheless, I had fabricated for myself, at least internally, an identity as writer, though it would be years before I fully understood what being a writer, what writing, really meant.

More than anything, I wanted to read, and I wanted someone to pay me to do this—to remunerate me for simply sitting around and reading. That was the position I was waiting to be offered. In fact, I had lost my job at the toy warehouse because I had built a hideout from enormous toy boxes in the top rack of shelves, against the torrid warehouse ceiling, and perched all day five stories above four acres of concrete reading Dostoevsky (I made it all the way through *The Idiot* before the axe fell), eating junior mints, and deviled crab from Munch's Lunch truck until it was time to punch out and head for beer at Sam and Ann's Bar.

I don't suppose I wanted the job laboring for my uncle, but among my male cousins, and my uncles, carrying a hod for Leo at least one summer of your life was the measure of your backbone, a family rite of passage, the spurs of manhood. Even my father had labored on a few occasions for Uncle Leo when he was on strike from the mill. So I cobbled together for myself a durable tale, something to mythologize what was sure to be agony: that the kind of work I was about to enter into— carrying a hod, whatever a hod was—was noble and honest. In truth, keenly romantic. Working construction was men's work: outside, under the sun, no shirt, khakis, clodhoppers, and a Pirates baseball cap. I had been an athlete all my life, and was in terrific physical shape.

What's more, I was 22 years old, a grown man, by anyone's calculation, a man who could handle whatever hardship a day's wages blew his way, one of Kerouac's exulted *fellaheen*, a chap who fit clearly the Hemingway code. I might be suffering internally, but I would never cry out. Hubris and ignorance, not to mention falsehood, are often all we have; and, as Camus points out in "The Myth of Sisyphus," "there is no fate that cannot be surmounted by scorn." Camus also reminds us in that perfect little essay that the Gods "had thought with some reason that there is no more dreadful punishment than futile and hopeless labor." Something that rang so witheringly true, even the first time I read it as a sixteen year old high school junior, and precisely what I sought to escape by leaving Pittsburgh.

My first day on the job was unbearable—much worse than I could have imagined. A day filled with shame, a textbook lesson in humility. My strength, my stamina, my intelligence, what I regarded as my superiority, ended up not being worth a bent nail. Before I stepped on that construction site that first day at 6:45 a.m., I had no idea what a hod was. Nevertheless, my entire life the word had been embedded in the family lexicon, a redolent symbol, seared into my collective unconscious. These days, I'm certain, hods are for the most part obsolete.

According to Webster's, a hod is *an open box attached to a long pole in which bricks or mortar are carried on the shoulder.* I find this an oversimplified definition, but adequate. The box is really a wedge one loads with bricks or mortar, then assumes on one's trapezoid the sharp weighted angle of the V, balancing the entire affair with a pole the length of a hoe handle, and totters across the pocked and littered site toward the bricklayers screaming at you to *hurry the fuck up.*

I loaded my first hod full of oozing mortar, situated myself at the hod stand as if assuming a brace of barbells to press, and stepped away with it on my shoulder. It was precisely like having a hundred pounds of concrete loaded into your skull, and a giraffe's center of gravity. Like a drunkard, I staggered for a moment, a slurry of mortar spilling over my face and torso, then managed before I toppled to get it racked back in the stand. I took a few more cracks at the hod, the bricklayers yapping unmercifully for me to hustle, but I just couldn't finesse it. The physics, not to mention the necessary Herculean strength, were too befuddling. I found a couple of five gallon metal buckets, shoveled them full of mortar and, one in each hand, humped mud like that all day. My attempt to transport bricks in the hod was equally pathetic, so I ended up using brick tongs, a clamped span of ten bricks in each hand.

Of course, the bricklayers and the other laborers made fun of me—Leo's nephew, some sissy college kid. The day was sheer misery, a horrifying soul-searing workout. By 3:30, quitting time, I was a mess, like I had been worked over under the hot blistering sun by a squad of nuns. More than anything, I was terrified I'd have to quit, simply give up, the kind of admission I don't think I ever could have come to grips with. I didn't know how I'd be able to last the summer. The disgrace of it all, the death blow to my early manhood, would have been too much to bear. But, day by day, lurch by lurch, I got the hang of it, and became a tolerable laborer, and even developed the kind of masochistic affection for it that one sometimes feels upon finishing a race that nearly kills you.

After going steady all day with the hod, I drove home; and, still in my sodden work clothes, jumped on a borrowed ten speed, and pedaled miles through the city streets, took a shower, and ate supper with my parents—one notch less in the numbered days we had left together under the same roof. My father, a millwright on the open hearth at Edgar Thomson Steel Works, in Braddock, PA, the first steel mill Andrew Carnegie had opened in America, arrived home by 4:30. A swell cook, he had supper on the table when my mother, a seamstress, downtown, in Brooks Brothers tailor shop, barged in from the bus stop, laden with packages and a chip on her shoulder. Like me, she bristled at authority.

Wednesday evenings I showed up in my dusty, mortar-encrusted laborer's clothes at Pitt's Cathedral of Learning for my three-hour seminar. Dr. Mooney bought his pristine shirts, his suits and blazers at Brooks Brothers. My mother might have basted his cuffs or taken in his trousers. His club ties matched his argyles. His wing-tips were blinding. Half-glasses sat at the tip of his long nose. Unabashedly wed to literature, he fulminated and sighed and theatrically read long passages from the texts—"miracles of compression," "marvels of economy"— to the class. Six-foot-five, willowy as Prince Myshkin, he often shot his French cuffs like a pool shark or hitman, but he was gentle, a purist, a dead ringer for Walter Matthau. It seems obvious now that Dr. Mooney was my inspiration for teaching— though sitting in his class, back then, clad in the honest filth of my peasant forbears, imagining myself in his robes, or possessing even a jot of his intellect, was as fantastic as the books on my syllabus.

The other grad students, much older than I, PhD candidates among whom I felt inferior—their vocabularies were exquisitely superior, inanely intoxicating—stared at me, I imagined, cowled in a cloud of brick and mortar dust, like I was a janitor instead of a working class hero. I never felt I belonged among them. The same way I felt among those bricklayers and carpenters, plumbers and electricians.

Occasional evenings, I hung out with my best friends (still my best friends), like brothers, neighborhood kids I'd known all my life, and gone through Catholic school and played ball with. Even then, my love for them was complete. Finally old enough to drink legally, after all those years of fake IDs, and Pittsburgh dives in the University district that served toddlers if they were tall enough to plunk their pennies on the bar, we'd split a cheap pitcher at Lou's Lounge or Taylor's. I can't remember a thing we said, just the scraps of their voices I embellish in fictive dialogue I invent in stories and poems, and it is often there within those pages that they live for me most poignantly. Or if I was feeling maudlin and profound, if the muse was teasing me—along with the fact then, as always, I was secretly in love and tongue-tied and jilted in the bargain—I'd drive to the dark smoky Mardi Gras, play sad songs by Graham Nash and Joni Mitchell on its kaleidoscopic jukebox and drink—at the bar, of course (the booths were for others)—exactly two very cold bottles of Schmidt's of Philadelphia. Laboring kept me in a state of constant thirst. Beer never tasted so good.

Sunday mornings, I played a softball double-header in an industrial league in played-out steel neighborhoods across the Monongahela River. I had put together a team—the *Deer*, just *Deer*—comprised of those same old friends, some of whom knew the game and played it well, and some who didn't. The team was a lark, a kind of absurdist flourish to my last summer in Pittsburgh where playing ball—baseball above all—had meant more to me than anything else. Baseball, even before books, had been my first dream. But, that summer I was about to turn twenty-three, it all began to fade on those treacherous oily fields grouted with glass and gravel, playing against guys who looked more like hung-over nose-guards than baseball players. They grunted when they rocketed their boozy homers over rusted two story chain link into the dingy cobblestone streets of Beechview and Carrick. They beat us to death and talked shit in the bargain: *Deer*. Whatever the hell that meant. And our foppish too-nice uniforms. We won three games and laughed our asses off. Egotistically orchestrating my own swan song, I kept stats and played as if my life depended on it.

Most nights I stayed home. My father read the newspaper. My mother with needle and thread. She had taken up quilting. The TV would be on. Eventually, it put them to sleep. Jimmy

Carter was running for president. Ford was a good guy. Nixon, deposed and disgraced, in the words of my mother, was "a sneaky bastard." I'd sit and have ice cream with them, a cup of tea—already I'd begun to despise television—then climb the stairs to my bedroom, still decked with the prizes of my boyhood: trophies and pennants, the mammoth poster of Babe Ruth above my bed, orbiting it small cameos of Muhammad Ali, Roberto Clemente, Ernest Hemingway and F. Scott Fitzgerald, the "romantic egoist." The requisite crucifix lent the room a churchy air. Congregated atop my dresser were statues of the Blessed Mother, the Sacred Heart, Saints Joseph, Francis, and Anthony, scapulars and Easter palm.

I climbed between the immaculate sheets—my mother still made my bed—and read about the boiling heat of Garcia-Marquez's Macondo, where characters thrived on meals of damp soil, spat butterflies, levitated. Where a "very old man" with "enormous wings," a "flesh-and-blood angel," plummets to earth one day and is locked in a chicken coop. Where the unearthly inexplicable is married to the mundane, and wholly unastonished by the union. I was forced to stop reading Carlos Fuentes' *The Death of Artemio Cruz.* It made me feel, I swear, like jagged pieces of metal were grinding inside me.

Latin American Literature was like acid: disorienting, inebriating, spiriting me off to the realm of *magical realism*—a term (whatever it means), as I remember, yet to be coined in 1976. Literary hallucinogens that made me lust to write. Though I never wrote. Maybe a scribble on a bar napkin that never made it out of my pocket. In the main, I read the Latin Americans and fell asleep early, sometimes chancing a cigarette in the candlelight of my boyhood, though my mother would give me hell about it the next day. *What was this VISTA bullshit anyway?* She was brokenhearted that I was leaving. My father too, though he said nothing, thank God, as was his wont. I had to be up at 5:30 every morning and drive to the site in my black VW bug with no reverse and work under the merciless sun carrying hods of brick and mortar. Real work.

That summer, I was preparing, I thought, to walk away from my past. I was leaving for VISTA (Volunteers in Service to America) and glad about it, and that pleasure, the joyous anticipation, at contemplating my escape from home and my family filled me with guilt. And my dear parents? How odd I must have seemed to them, in the last days of my life as an only child—my older sister, Marie, had married six years earlier—the first person with my surname to graduate from college; and now, by God, getting a Master's Degree in English Literature—whatever that was—then traipsing off to work in a prison 500 miles away.

Fridays, after work, I drove straight home and left my battered work boots at the back door with the three other pairs queued on the stoop and walked in the kitchen. Around the table were my dad, then only 61; my Godfather, Paul Pagano (my dad was Paul's Godfather); and my cousin-through-marriage, Paul's son-in-law, Ronnie Villani.

Paul was a cement finisher, son of a cement finisher who had emigrated from Napoli and my dad's eldest sister, Vincenza. Paul looked like Tyrone Power. At age 17, two weeks after high school graduation, he was drafted, and sent to Naval Basic and Boot Camp. Weeks later, he boarded the USS North Carolina, Battleboat 55, the most decorated sea-faring vessel during World World II, then hurtled across the Pacific to join the fleet for the invasion of Japan—though the bombs were dropped on Hiroshima and Nagasaki while he was en route.

Ronnie had grown up on Lenora Street, behind Larimer Field. He'd played for Pete D'Imperio's famous '64 City League single-wing champs at Westinghouse High. The only white kid on the all-black team. The only white kid in his all-black graduating class. All-City tackle. Stronger than Samson. Big and hairy and beneficent. Beautiful teeth. He worked heavy construction. Sheetrock up and down eighty stories, all day, with his bare hands.

Quiet, steady, my dad rose daily in the dark, packed my lunch—and my mother's—still scribbled in pencil my name on the little brown bag, brewed a thermos of coffee for me, often left a few bucks under my stash or in the front seat of my VW. By the time I stepped on the site at 6:45—wearing his boots and gloves, his hat, his name—he'd been long punched in, sweltering at the mouth of a blast furnace, or belted to a boom crane gantry high above the Monongahela.

They were the men I wanted to be like. Dr. Mooney too.

The four of us were shirtless and brown. Crosses on chains glinted on our tanned chests. Along with his cross, Ronnie sported the tribal horn to ward off the *malocchio*, the evil eye. On the table gleamed the bottle of Black Velvet, twinkling amber in the late afternoon sun like an icon itself at quitting time. Squat sweating bottles of cold Iron City in front of each of them to chase the shots, canted neatly in cordial glasses. Piled in a platter were provolone and salami, olives and tomatoes, fresh Sicilian bread my dad had purchased at dawn at Rimini's down on Larimer Avenue. A cast iron vat of hot sausage and peppers, my dad's specialty, simmered on the stove. The screen door was open. The summer birds sang in Italian.

When I disappeared from that kitchen thirty-seven years ago, and walked onto a North Carolina prison yard, into the wildly new, unlikely life awaiting me—and later into a college classroom where I would make my living and vocation—I left behind the harrowing necessity, the tradition of my family as far back as anyone can reckon, of literally sweating and dangerously punishing my body in crud and abysmal weather to score a paycheck. I became a teacher and writer, a man with soft hands, pressed shirts, clean shoes I no longer had to check at the back door. The dream of my ancestors when they hobbled onto those ships along Italy's impoverished coast, possessed of tools, bread, and the clothes on their backs, was that I and my ilk would never know what William Faulkner calls, in "A Rose for Emily," "the old thrill and the old despair of a penny more or less." I don't even know how to be thankful enough that I stumbled into this life of books, this "last good job in America." It is a catechism lesson in the undeserved gift of grace, in all its lustrous numen.

Yet the instinct toward manual labor, that Calvinist bent of mortifying the flesh—nailed to my pysche, to my very soul, by a brace of galvanized ten-pennies—still nags me. I find myself addled with a sense of unworthiness if I do not submit daily to a ritual of self-imposed physical hardship. Other than the usual house maintenance—the occasional coat of paint, habitual grass-cutting, weed-eating, snow-shoveling, keeping the cars roadworthy, animal husbandry, etc.—how does the garden-variety English Professor-Writer sublimate such a compulsion? A kind of guilt arising from the suspicion that a life of the mind exclusively, unleavened by blue collar toil, is not quite enough? That it leads, perhaps, to a spiritual quandary?

150

I run a lot of miles, every day, regardless of geography or weather, and I pray as I log them, reflexively, as if storing up the kinds of indulgences—as instructed by the nuns who savagely taught me—that will whittle time off my de rigueur jolt in Purgatory. Running is no-nonsense work without a whit of glamor—often painful, most of the time uncomfortable, glorious in not very obvious ways, but glorious nonetheless. Ever the poet, Saint Paul said it nicely in II Corinthians: *Wherefore we labour, that, whether present or absent, we may be accepted of Him.* The worst indictment I ever heard from my father was when he would say of another man, "He's so lazy he stinks."

My dad, Paul, and Ronnie: they smiled when I appeared at the threshold. These were my people and, on Friday afternoons, strolling into my parents' kitchen, as if out of the boiling shimmer of Macondo, grimy and happy that my week with the hod and the grad students was over, I had become a *manovale*, a real worker, like the men of my family. My dad jumped up and fetched me a beer. Paul poured me a shot. Ronnie clapped me on the back—like being smacked with a sack of mortar—and proclaimed, "My man."

They laughed. How the hell was I going to make out on the two grand a year and food stamps I'd be making as a VISTA? I couldn't have learned too much with all that college. Then they really laughed. I laughed too. I didn't know how the hell I'd make out. In just a few weeks I'd be on a prison yard. I'd have a Cuban room-mate whose father was locked in Castro's jail. I'd tour Death Row, then the gas chamber. I'd fall precipitously in love with a woman from Georgia and marry her fourteen months later. I'd engage for the rest of my life the habitual sustained toil, the real work, of writing. Traipsing out

151

of one world, through a secret portal, and lurching into another.

Together we lifted the shots—*Saluto*—threw them back and chased them with an Iron.

Half of What I Say Is Meaningless

A few summers ago, my family and I packed up our household and moved a mere 1.4 miles down the road. Among my horde of haphazard papers, I discovered an old catalog and application from McGill University in Canada. Its envelope was postmarked *Montreal, Quebec, 22 Feb '72* and addressed to me at California State College, in the little southwestern Pennsylvania coal town of California, where I was then enrolled as a freshman. This little brown package is the only extant artifact of my brush with the Vietnam War.

For boys of my generation, Vietnam had been there all along, like some hideous lethal recessive gene, inching its celluloid way into our futures. When and how I became conscious of it I can't say. The sound and sight of its strange syllables—*Vietnam*—infiltrated households everywhere. It seemed as though the backdrop of my childhood and early teen years was a tacked-up sheet upon which played, like surreal home movies, the TV images of the war: a dreary black and white jungle scape, dream-like chaos; soldiers in camos being dragged by buddies; machine gun fire; explosions; and an odd foreshadowing vocabulary: *Saigon, Hue, Khesanh, TET, Danang, Camranh, Quantri, DMZ, Dakto, Ho Chi Minh.* What were these things? By the time I knew, they were indelibly napalmed into my consciousness. My future had arrived and, like most of my pals, I was politically vacuous. I packed up and went to college. My parents were picking up the tab.

The United States draft lottery for boys born in 1953, such as myself, took place during the first weeks of 1972. All 365 days of the year were dropped into the proverbial hat. The boys born on the first 150 or so dates plucked were sure to be drafted. Those with high numbers, 200 or above, were delivered. No draft. No war. No military of any kind. The ones who caught a 75 or lower could count on being sent to Vietnam. Student deferments had been abolished. I copped a 33. I was 18, home in Pittsburgh for the holidays, having successfully completed my first college semester (I had made the Dean's List). At the time, there were 140,000 American soldiers still fighting in Vietnam, half the number of twelve months before.

I was alone when I heard the news about my draft number over the radio. My mother and father were at their jobs as seamstress and steelworker. My sister was married. I wasn't shocked. I wasn't scared. I wasn't anything. But I knew I was changed, as if God had hit me over the head with this big, irrevocable random thing and I would never be the same. It only vaguely occurred to me that I could die. More than anything, it signaled in bold letters that I was no longer a child; that the charmed existence I had enjoyed thus far—that I figured would shield me forever—was a thing of the past. My mother and father, my aunts and uncles—no one could stand in the way of this. I was suddenly a man. I sat around the house and read, drank coffee—a privilege of being an adult—until it was time to hitchhike down to meet my girlfriend, who was still in high school.

On the steps of Sacred Heart gym, the gym where I had learned to play basketball, where I had taken my first shower, where I had noticed in eighth grade the first black hairs blooming out of my chest, I sat waiting for her, smoking cigarettes (I kept my smoking hidden from my parents) and listened to the hoops ringing with the girls' practice free throws. It was snowing. The sky was greyish purple. All the automobiles had their lights on, though it was only three o'clock. A gloomy day, the kind of Pittsburgh day I loved: a day when any minute the sky could unload enough snow to slow things to a crawl, then finally to a halt, and by nightfall there would be the feeling that time had stopped and nothing bad could ever happen.

The moment she saw me, my girlfriend started crying and threw herself into my arms. Like everyone else, she had heard the news. On the covers of her books were magic-markered peace signs. She wore dangly earrings, love beads and tiny skirts. She was only sixteen and fully intended to marry me.

"We'll go to Canada," she said.

At that moment, that plan suited me. I had no intention of entering the armed forces. In fact, I had no intentions whatsoever.

That night at supper my mother broke down and sobbed, though we never talked about my number. I realized how different, nearly tragic, I had become in the eyes of others. I had always wanted to be different—indeed had always thought myself so—but not like this.

When I returned to California State in for Spring Semester, I received the same treatment. Reactions varied from those who offered sympathy and commiseration to those who told me I was a dead man. And there were quite a few in between who asked me what I was going to do. I had no idea.

My girlfriend and I feverishly wrote letters back and forth. Our first plan was that I would apply for Conscientious Objector status. If that didn't work, our backup was Canada. We would get married, I would enter a Canadian university, then, according to plan, on to law school where I would become a lawyer who defended the poor and downtrodden. Chiseled into the bedrock of my mind was an unyielding picture of the future. I would grow a mustache, wear three piece suits, and practice law from home in a giant oak-paneled study where my gleaming, cuddly children would feel free to play, while I worked, until my wife called us to meals in the sunroom. It could be done, my girlfriend and I assured each other.

Without delay I sent off to McGill University for a catalog and application materials. Then, on a weekend home, I took a bus downtown to the Federal Building and picked up a form outlining procedures for obtaining CO status. The clerk who handed it to me explained all I had to do was write a statement.

A conscientious objector is against war for moral reasons. I believed the war was immoral. Everyone said so, especially those with whom, at least rhetorically, I had aligned myself. I was not a violent person. I absolutely did not believe in killing. Therefore I embodied all of the virtues of a conscientious objector, and felt absolved of any hypocrisy in claiming that status. I certainly had the clothes for it. That day, I wore a purple shirt, white and blue-striped bell bottoms with a macrame belt, work boots, an army jacket, in the pocket of which was Sartre's *The Age of Reason*. My shoulder-length hair flowed out from under a navy blue watch cap. I brimmed with confidence. Until I read the form.

To be classified as a conscientious objector you must be opposed to war in any form. Your objection must be based on moral or ethical beliefs, or beliefs which are commonly accepted as religious. Your beliefs must influence your life as the belief in God influences the life of one who is a traditionally religious conscientious objector. To qualify, your conscience must be spurred by deeply held moral, ethical or religious beliefs which would give you no peace if you allowed yourself to become a combatant member of the armed forces.

There were also a number of questions addressing the applicant's "core of beliefs." It was like applying for the priesthood. To simply pen "War and killing are bad"—which in 1972 was a bit of a cliché—would not be enough. And that's all I had in my arsenal. I needed an ideology, and there in the cold hall outside the draft board, I realized, with a touch of panic, that I thoroughly lacked one.

Looking for reassurance, I caught a bus and got off at The Friends Peace Center on Ellsworth Avenue in Oakland. There I explained to a long-haired, bearded counselor, whose job was to coach people like me, that I had scored a bum draft number and I wanted to shoot for a CO.

He gave me a withering look and asked what I would do if I walked in the door of my home and found someone raping my mother. I knew what the correct answer was. The true pacifist would somehow persuade the offender, in a completely nonviolent manner, to stop his assault. As I visualized the scenario, I saw myself reaching for the big knife my mother sliced eggplant with and stabbing the culprit as many times as I had to—and maybe even a few extra for good measure. I replied vaguely that I'd do whatever to protect my mother.

"You are probably not a CO," he said. I was still welcome, of course, to submit a statement to my draft board, but first I needed to spend some time reflecting on my commitment to peace and nonviolence.

I thanked him and walked out into the winter air. It was a dark, bitter day. Snow, wind, slush. People turned away from one another. I stuck out my thumb. No one stopped. I started walking. How disrespectful, how egotistical, to think that I could be a CO just by writing a statement. And, really, I wasn't "opposed to war in any form." The United States' involvement in World War II was crucial. As moral as it gets.

I was born in 1953, into the Republican presidency of Dwight Eisenhower, eight years after the Hiroshima and Naga-saki bombings. The Korean War armistice was signed when I was just seven days old. Joseph McCarthy busily wrecked the lives of innocent people. My entire extended family, actually every adult I knew, was still deranged from The Depression and World War II, and talked about them as if they had happened but the day before. War was an integral part of my collective unconscious. My father and uncles were veterans. I had grown up with a beloved arsenal of toy guns. Like other little boys of my generation, I adored any film with sword or gunplay. Had anyone asked me just a few years before I started college who my favorite actor was, I probably would have volunteered John Wayne. I had loved *The Green Berets*, propagandist pap through and through.

In truth, I had always thought of myself, in some pit of my subconscious, as a soldier. Before I ever heard of the war in Vietnam, I had lived through The Bay of Pigs and The Cuban Missile Crisis. I'd grown up during the height of the Cold War. Kruschev, Castro—these were dirty words. My entire existence was paramilitary, my psyche pocked with trenches and foxholes. Damn it, I was a boy, and there was nothing better and braver and truer and more blessed in the eyes of God and country than a soldier. Girls have babies. Boys go to war. Period. What was it our football coach told us? *Make them piss blood.*

Apparently I was not against killing and violence. I would have loved being a war hero. The reasons I didn't want to go to war were quite simple: It would be an epic interruption and I was afraid. As for my "belief in God," well, I realized I hadn't yet consulted Him. At the sobering announcement that my number was *33,* I had prayed for miraculous deliverance, but it seemed an eternity since I had gone to Mass or received the sacraments. I had no "deeply held moral, ethical or religious beliefs." I wasn't even sure what I believed any more.

So I went back to California and waited to hear from McGill. Lurking in my mail was a summons from the draft board. I was classified 1-A and was to report back to the Federal Building for my pre-induction physical. I did not tell my parents about the letter. I might even have thrown it away. I'm not sure. But what I am sure about is that I did not report for that physical.

When the materials for McGill arrived in late February of 1972, I was nearly a month into my second semester and doing well. In addition to my classes, I was on the dorm council and the varsity track team, and had even published, anonymously, a poem called "This Disgruntled Noise" (my first ever publication) in the campus literary magazine.

Living in a welter of new theories and ideas that college offered, I began to sense what a mechanized, futile place the world was, how technology subverts humanity at every turn, how instead of souls people now had appliances. In my beloved, imagined poverty, I fueled all-nighters with instant coffee whitened with Pream. I'd even started smoking a corncob pipe packed with flavored tobacco. I sat at my desk, puffing by candlelight, a stick of incense imbedded in the candle wax, and wrote poems that, I was sure, would one day bring me fame. My dorm buddies, mostly tough, edgy kids from one-horse steel towns in the Monongahela Valley, eyed me with respect. To them I was cool, intense, a real silver-plated egghead bookworm who would still chip in, even on school nights, for a couple quarts of Iron City beer.

My favorite teacher was a fellow named Connie Mack Rea, a former pro baseball player and direct descendant of legendary baseball pioneer, Connie Mack. A tall, enigmatic, ruggedly handsome man with a clipped mustache, he called us by our last names: *Mister* or *Miss*. He wore elaborately knit sweaters; leather; expensive sports jackets; pointy, tooled cowboy boots. His air was wholly aristocratic, vain, wry, condescending, perhaps even tragic, as if he were nursing some secret wound, about which he'd remain eternally silent.

There was a word Mr. Rea used frequently, though far from casually, a word I had heard kicked around in high school, and which had come to embody, among my friends and me, a superficial chic: *existentialism*. I never really knew what it meant, but would mouth it occasionally as a kind of password. Even now I've had to consult Webster's to get my bearings. Pinning it down is like trying to scoop Mercury. Mr. Rea described it as the primal core of individuality, the insideness of you and you alone that no one—physicians, priests, parents, lovers, no one—could get at or near because your minute by minute experience placed you in a category of one.

No wonder I had been feeling so misunderstood all my life. By God, I had been born an existentialist. And never had I felt so misunderstood than at the moment my birth date betrayed me. How could anyone know how I felt? What it was like to look into my own personal abyss? Heck, even I didn't know what it was like, and it was my abyss.

In Mr. Rea's class, I read Albert Camus's "The Myth of Sisyphus," an essay of just over a thousand words that seemed to sum it all up: Step out of line and, like Sisyphus, the absurd hero, you are given a rock that, every time you finally roll it up the mountain, rolls back down. The gods, Camus writes, "had thought with some reason that there is no more dreadful punishment than futile and hopeless labor."

Existentialism seemed the perfect posture for a fellow in my spot. The notion that life is meaningless, at best a cruel joke, made perfect sense. I was ready to sign on, though I was far from a nihilist. In fact, I was hopelessly ambitious, and rather confident. I had goals. I studied like mad so I'd get all A's in my courses. Existentialists don't give a damn about A's. Absurdist heroes don't study. Goals are mere illusions. But I also liked being different, and even though I didn't clearly understand it at the time, existentialism supplied me with a kind of defense mechanism. Meanwhile, sitting prominently on my dorm room desk, for all to see, was my application from McGill, waiting to be filled out and sent back to Montreal.

My year at California ended in May of 1972. The United States had mined Haiphong Harbor and stepped up its bombing of North Vietnam. It looked like the war would never end. I still had not reported for my induction physical.

I never applied to McGill. I guess I never really intended to. The enormity of leaving home, family, friends, country, and the only life I'd ever known to begin study at a Canadian university must have finally sunk in. I didn't have a car. I didn't have money. I didn't speak French. I hadn't even talked to my parents about it. What I had done is transfer my existential A's from California State to the University of Pittsburgh, less than five miles from the house where I'd grown up, the house I would begin living in again after a year of absolute freedom.

Mere days before Fall classes began at Pitt, I received another notice for my physical. This time the language was explicit: Get down there pronto or get in serious trouble. Period.

How the idea of ROTC, and the instant deferment it would furnish me with, filtered into my head, I don't know. Someone must have suggested it to me. The very thought of ROTC, what I regarded as its Mickey Mouse lockstep idiocy, repelled me. The stupid uniforms, drilling, the caricatured nauseating patriotism, the lack of cynicism—it all seemed designed to thwart existentialism at every turn. But I needed a deferment in a hurry. The Selective Service was breathing down my neck. I was close to treason.

Out of this new turn I constructed yet another romanticized vision of myself: the dashing army officer and his lovely wife. After ROTC and graduation, the United States government would pay for my law school. I'd repay them with a few years of service, then retreat back to counterculture with a carload of army money I'd saved. It seemed a smart plan. I simply added this vision, with an asterisk and a footnote, to the earlier one of myself in the paneled office with the wife and kids.

My Pitt ID card, fall of 1972, shows a fellow who, with his long brown hair resting on his shoulders, looks nothing like a brand new ROTC cadet. Nevertheless, sliding into ROTC was simple. All I did was take the elevator up to one of the spooky, marble floors in the Cathedral of Learning—interestingly enough the same floor where gay men were rumored to tryst in one of the rest rooms—and talk for a few minutes to the campus commander, a jolly, old, craggy colonel with medals and cigarette ashes spread all over his olive uniform. He was delighted to have me. My grades were superior; I seemed like an honorable, serious young man. I'd make a fine officer. We shook hands repeatedly. I signed a few forms.

Then the colonel took me to an adjacent room where I met two lean, young, handsome, cigarette-smoking officers who taught in the program: one black, one white, Vietnam combat vets, immaculately clipped, pressed, starched, and decorated. Like a magazine ad for the grand Republic's armies, their very presence denied that there could ever be a moment's mayhem on the globe while men like them stood guard. They welcomed me to the ranks, and squashed my hand in theirs. I figured I could handle ROTC. No one had even mentioned my hair. Across the Atlantic, the Paris Peace Talks languished.

Later that day, along with my two ROTC courses—U.S. Defense Establishment and Survey of American Military Theory—I registered for African-American History, Comparative Literature in 20th Century Narrative, Seminar in Van Gogh, Dramatic Literature, and (oh, yes) Existentialism.

That first semester at Pitt, I majored in being two people at once. Foremost, I was a fire-breathing, liberated student, ingesting books, scholarship and the world around him, frequently without even chewing. I trotted euphorically class to class, Nietzsche, Kierkegaard, Heidegger whispering cryptically in my ear.

Leaning out of my seat in Existentialism, coffee in one hand, a pen in the other, and a Newport dangling existentially out of my mouth, I recorded every word Dr. Nehamas uttered. A Greek with a huge head of wiry hair, he strolled the lecture hall, wreathed in cigarette smoke, lighting one filterless Lucky after another. I understood Existentialism less than I had the year before, but at least had its vocabulary down pat.

I read, I studied, I went to see Fellini movies. I made a science of the epigraph and proved that with a little synthesis one could get A after A simply by stringing together one brilliant quote after another. It was even possible to delude yourself and your friends that you had thought of these things yourself. Books were like drugs. If someone mentioned a title, I wrote it down and combed the city until it was mine, even if I didn't always get around to reading it. I developed an additional vision of my future self: working in a modest little office where all I had to do was read books and no one ever checked on me. What I really wanted was to be was a writer, but I figured I could fit that in when I wasn't in a courtroom rescuing (free of charge, of course) some helpless victim—that is, after I had paid the United States government back with four years of my life.

The other me was the ROTC cadet. Though I was a model student in my other classes, I was mediocre to poor in my Military Science courses, which didn't count toward my grade point average. I became increasingly sloppy about them: daydreaming, cutting classes, exuding a less than positive attitude. I didn't like my teachers: the white guy and the black guy. Their pedagogy tended to spill over into personal accounts of Vietnam: "greasing gooks," "dustoffs," "KIAs," and so on. In fact, my sudden proximity to the military only galvanized my antipathy for it. I didn't like my crew-cut fellow cadets either. They didn't seem like tough Army guys—more like the pasty types who sit on their porches all summer playing Risk, and paging through *The Rise and Fall of the Third Reich*. Nerdy, sexist, giggly, they were so bloody clean and unctuous and certain about everything. Not an existentialist among them.

On occasion all cadets were required to assemble at Pitt Stadium for full-dress drills. On such days, the other cadets wore their uniforms, festooned with nifty patches and insignia, around campus. I kept mine crammed into a duffle bag, then donned it, pitifully rumpled, in the privacy of the locker room before stepping onto the stadium AstroTurf for the hour and a half of marching, screaming, and saluting. How idiotic I looked in that hateful uniform, the heavy officer's cap clamped over my long, flowing hair. After drills I'd hustle back to the locker room, climb into my bells and T-shirt, and wad that uniform back into the bag, tamping it down with my *Viking Portable Nietzsche*.

One day, the white officer told me that he'd like to see me in his office later that afternoon. I showed up with a copy of Andre Breton's famous surrealist novel, *Nadja*, which we'd been tackling in Comparative Literature. To cap it off, I had just finished watching, mere minutes before, Bunuel's deranged film, *Un Chien Andalou*. I was fairly thrumming with "unnatural juxtapositions and combinations." Life's decided lack of meaning had never been more manifest.

The white officer rose when I came in, squished my hand in his, smiled warmly and motioned me to sit. He sat back down, propped his feet on his desk, and lit a cigarette. For a protracted moment, he simply beamed at me, and I did my best to beam back. His office walls were spread with action photos of him and other soldiers, plaques, citation after citation. On his desk were pictures of his wife and two small sons, dressed in army uniforms. Above his head, the American flag drooped.

"What's with the hair?" he asked, still smiling.

"Nothing," I said.

"You some kind of hippie?"

"No."

"No, what?"

"No, sir."

"Do you think you are tough?"

On his second cigarette, he still smiled, smoke now shrouding both of us. We were apparently making a surreal movie, but no one had bothered telling me. He was certainly following the format: a series of non sequiturs. I felt like the eyeball slit by the razor in Bunuel's opening scene. In keeping with the surreal tenor of things, I considered launching into a bout of meaningless laughter. Perhaps I could get drummed out for mental instability. A permanent deferral. What they called a "Section 8" on *McHale's Navy*. But I was too pissed to laugh. About the whole thing. My lottery number, the war, ROTC. The fact that I had to sit there and take shit from this martinet on whom I could smell the violence and apocalyptic fever of war. Maybe that was his game: to get me angry, to motivate me.

"I don't want to come down too hard on you, but you have to get more involved. These cadets are a great group of guys, and you're missing out on a lot of opportunities. And fun." He stood up. "Whatta you say?" That smile was still nailed to his face.

"Yeah," I said.

He tilted his head and kind of smirked.

"Yes, sir," I amended.

"There you go."

He stuck out his hand and I squeezed back as hard as I could.

"And how about a haircut?" Then he winked.

News from Paris, where Henry Kissinger and Le Duc Tho had been tussling over an armistice for nearly three years, was by turns hopeful and grim. America, after years of fighting in Vietnam, remained pessimistic, and so did I. The only hope for peace rested with George McGovern, the Democratic presidential candidate in 1972. Like Eugene McCarthy before him, he had underpinned his campaign with the promise of unilateral withdrawal of American troops from Southeast Asia. On November 7, voting for the first time in a presidential election, I prayerfully cast my vote for McGovern, an act of high treason for an ROTC cadet. With McGovern in the White House, I could quit ROTC and get back to my life full-time. With my parents, lifelong Democrats, I watched election returns as long as I could bear it. Nixon by a landslide. Absolute murder.

A few days later, my parents received a letter from the Colonel informing them that on November 15, during a public ceremony at the university, I would be one of the ROTC cadets receiving an award for "outstanding academic performance." The letter went on to say that

> the United States Army possesses more complicated equipment than ever before, and must employ increasingly complex personnel to intelligently maintain and manage these resources. It is particularly important that we find responsible young leaders for this task—men, who, like your son, have demonstrated intellectual abilities noticeably above their contemporaries. In qualifying for this award, your son has demonstrated such competence. We are quite proud to have in him the Cadet Battalion.

My parents were pleased, ridiculously so. I wanted to attack them. Or at least point out the exquisite irony that I was not being "honored" for having achieved superior grades in my Military Science classes, but in those that championed radical politics, subversive thinking, civil disobedience, and revolution. Had I been able to intercept the letter, I would have ripped it to bits, incinerated it, spat and stomped upon it. An onionskin, what looked like a carbon at that, not even letterhead, the Colonel hadn't even signed it. No telling who had written it. Its pompous rhetoric was precisely why I was in a pickle. *Increasingly complex personnel.* What was I? A robot? *Responsible young leaders.* Please! Who the hell was he talking about? *Battalion.* God! I wasn't going to any damned ceremony.

Incredulous, my parents watched me flop and rant. They thought I was having a nervous breakdown. When I got around to reconsidering my position—I was being extorted, of course—I knew I had to suck it up and show up for the award. Not only that. After seeing myself in the mirror in full uniform, with the long hair, cap and all—looking more like Tiny Tim than Custer—I headed for the barber shop. By my standards, the haircut was a massacre. But by the army's, even though the barber had chopped off a foot, it counted for little. My hair still covered my neck and ears. I was desolate. My girlfriend assured me it was "cute." My mother said grudgingly, "It looks nice." My father neglected to comment.

Thank God, it was an evening affair, so I had cover of darkness to conceal me in my uniform. As I walked onstage with my most unsoldierly, shaggy head to receive my award—a rectangle of heavy stock paper with "Certificate of Achievement" scrolled across its top—I imagined a hush come over the audience, their heads shaking in approbation. The Colonel, as he shook my hand, mispronounced my name. It had also been spelled incorrectly on the certificate. The other cadets glowered at me; my inability to conform had become insupportable. I couldn't stand much more. Yet as much as I despised them, and disdained their approval, I secretly craved it too. My unconscious still insisted that the cut of a man is measured by whether he can soldier or not.

As a photographer snapped pictures and the audience applauded—my proud, befuddled, probably embarrassed parents among them—the torrid stage lights grilled me like an inquisitor, revealing every flaw I possessed. I couldn't make out the audience for the glare. But I knew they were out there in the black, crouched in ambush like Vietcong, and this was perhaps my last moment on earth. Maybe I would, for one searing moment, see or know just one thing clearly before the lights went down and the hall emptied forever.

But I saw nothing. Only the hollow place inside me where my soul should have been. Then that space began to fill with those boys who had gone to Vietnam: terrified, exhausted ghosts tripping along jungle trails, scared kids my age, who had stepped up for me, who had had their lives blasted to pieces, fighting in my place, so that I could remain safe. There they marched, with the grit of my forebears who had never side-stepped wars. Above all, I was ashamed. Not only was I not worthy of the uniform, I lacked the conviction to be a CO. Even as an existentialist I was an impostor, nothing more than a pampered dilettante. The applause coursed over me, wave after wave, until it finally chased me out the door. When my mother and father caught up, I was in the backseat of the car, like a child, tearing myself out of that uniform. My identity, like dandelion fluff, had blown off in a hundred directions. I didn't know it at the time, but I had achieved existentialist status. And it was horrible.

I finished my first term at Pitt with a 3.6 GPA. I ended up with a B and a C in my two Military Science classes. A week before Christmas, Nixon unleashed the most significant air attack against North Vietnam since the war had started. On Christmas day, as my family and I sat down to feast, American bombers over Hanoi and Haiphong dropped death by the ton. Even though U.S. troop strength in Vietnam was at an all-time low, there seemed no reason to believe the war would ever end.

When the new college term began in the bitter cold mid-January of 1973, I signed up for only one Military Science course: First Basic Army. I skipped the first few classes. I never wanted to walk into one of those classrooms, or see any of those people, again. I was simply stalling before resuming my masquerade, waiting to be rescued by some miracle that would never materialize.

As a second semester sophomore, it was time for me to officially declare a major. I had always listed my major as Political Science simply because it was considered an advantageous pre-law curriculum. Looking over my transcripts, I realized that at the end of the year I would have thirty hours in English and Comparative Literature, nearly enough to satisfy degree requirements. I had taken an introductory course in Political Science. Nothing else. The next day I declared myself an English major. I could still go to law school, but for the short run, I wouldn't have to torture myself with courses I didn't care about. I'd do what came naturally, with great joy and passion. Unabashed, I'd read books, and maybe even write a few someday, which is what I really wanted. I was still pushing that boulder up the mountain, but a little bit of it fell away when I admitted what I loved.

The better part of that rock, however, remained. I still hadn't set foot in my ROTC class. Ducking into alcoves and bathrooms, crossing streets whenever I encountered the other cadets and the Military Science professors, I felt like a fugitive. AWOL. I had my beloved books, but they could not protect me from the draft. Canada crossed my mind again and again. I still had the application from McGill. On Monday—it was still very early in the term—I'd go back to ROTC classes, lie and beg forgiveness, take my medicine. Everything would be okay.

Saturday, January 27, I was working for a flower shop, pulling dead flowers out of a synagogue where the Torah was exposed. I wandered up onto the altar and stared at it with absolutely no comprehension. It was a miserable, gray day: no sun, frigid, dirty snow banked high at the curbs, sickly flakes withering down.

Feeling pretty sorry for myself, I turned on the radio of the 1969 Volkswagen microbus, which smelled of dead cigars and funerals. John Lennon sang, ever so plaintively: *Half of what I say is meaningless.* From "Julia," a song inspired by his mother. Precisely at the word *meaningless,* the song went dead, and an excited voice, clearly not Lennon's, announced that peace accords had been formally signed in Paris. The Vietnam War was over. The United States would no longer enforce a draft.

I lingered a moment, staring out the window, wondering if what I had heard could possibly be true. It was. The radio, on every band, verified it again and again. The war was indeed over, and I would not have to go to Vietnam, or be in the army, or take an induction physical, or ever go to another ROTC class again.

How strange to receive such miraculous news alone in a frozen synagogue parking lot. I turned off the radio and nudged the bus into first, skidding across the consecrated ice. Lennon's lyrics lodged in my head like scripture. Navigating my dangerous hometown streets, I sang those same seven words over and over—ringed by a chorus of snowy dead soldiers no older than I.